Improving Teacher Quality

Improving Teacher Quality

THE U.S. TEACHING FORCE
IN GLOBAL CONTEXT

Motoko Akiba and Gerald LeTendre

Teachers College, Columbia University
New York and London

To Fumie Kobayashi

Sister and dedicated teacher

and

Chihiro Yamada, Kazuyo Yamaguchi, and Teruyo Kitajima

Mentors and outstanding teachers

Published by Teachers College Press, 1234 Amsterdam Avenue, New York, NY 10027

Portions of Chapter 3 are reprinted from "Teacher Quality, Opportunity Gap, and National Achievement in 46 Countries," by M. Akiba, G. LeTendre, and J. P. Scribner, *Educational Researcher, 36*(7), pp. 369–387, copyright © 2007, by Sage Publications, Inc. Reprinted by permission of SAGE Publications.

Library of Congress Cataloging-in-Publication Data

Akiba, Motoko.
    Improving teacher quality : the U.S. teaching force in global context / Motoko Akiba and Gerald LeTendre.
        p.   cm.
    Includes bibliographical references and index.
    ISBN 978-0-8077-4988-3 (pbk : alk. paper)
    1. Teachers—In-service training—Cross-cultural studies.   2. Teacher effectiveness—Cross-cultural studies.   3. Teachers—Rating of—Cross-cultural studies.   I. LeTendre, Gerald K.   II. Title.

    LB1731.A435 2009
    371.1'44—dc22

                                                            2009007238

ISBN: 978-0-8077-4988-3 (paper)

Printed on acid-free paper
Manufactured in the United States of America

16   15   14   13   12   11   10   09   8   7   6   5   4   3   2   1

Contents

Acknowledgments

A NUMBER OF people contributed to our work. For our study on teacher policy in Japan, we would like to thank Professor Kazuhiko Shimizu at the University of Tsukuba; Dr. Masaaki Hayo and Dr. Teruyuki Fujita at the National Education Policy Research Center in the Ministry of Education, Culture, Sports, Science and Technology; Mr. Hiroyuki Kurata at the Tsukuba Board of Education; and Professor Hodaka Fujii at Tokyo Gakugei University. Our work would not have been possible without the contributions of many people in Australia. We appreciate the help of Professor Jill Blackmore at Deakin University; Professor Debra Hayes at the University of Sydney; Dr. Lawrence Ingvarson at the Australian Council for Educational Research; Mr. Paul Martin at the New South Wales Institute of Teachers; Ms. Ann Taylor and Mr. Justin Mullaly at the Australian Education Union Victorian Branch; Mr. Andrew Ius at the Victoria Institute of Teaching; and Ms. Diane Wasson in Human Resource Policy and Planning and Ms. Frances Plummer in the NSW AGQTP office in the New South Wales Department of Education and Training. We also would like to thank a number of teachers and administrators with whom we communicated during our visits to Japan and Australia and many U.S. teachers, school administrators, and district officers whom we interviewed in previous work that led to this book. All of these people were patient and kind in providing information and sharing their insights and perspectives on teacher policy. Finally, we thank Professor Margaret Grogan at Claremont Graduate University and Professor Jay P. Scribner at the University of Missouri-Columbia for critical feedback and insights on an earlier draft.

Introduction

IMPROVING TEACHER QUALITY has become the educational mantra of the new millennium. The passage of the No Child Left Behind (NCLB) Act in 2002 has set off a flurry of debate about defining and refining the appropriate mechanism for improving teacher quality, yet interventions often take the form of mandates on teacher entry requirements without corresponding support for improving teachers' professional learning opportunities and working conditions. While the American scholarly and political debates take place as if the United States were an isolated case, in fact the United States debates and reforms are simply part of a larger, long-term global trend toward more standardization and accountability in the public schooling sector. Accountability and standards-based reforms are worldwide phenomena affecting national systems of education and teachers.

This global trend to accentuate accountability and standards-based reforms has led many countries to develop and implement national policies for improving teacher quality, and has been the impetus for the search for "best practices" in teaching on a global scale. While teachers abroad, as in the United States, often are held accountable for student learning outcomes, countries vary significantly in terms of how they support teachers in improving their instructional practices, their lifelong development as professionals, as well as their working conditions. While it is often difficult to transfer teaching practices from one culture to another, countries can learn a great deal from the successes and failures of national policies designed to affect the teacher workforce as a whole. A careful cross-national comparative study can inform future directions of U.S. policies for improving teacher quality, by identifying major policies implemented in other nations and analyzing their impact.

A GLOBAL POLICY PERSPECTIVE

This book provides just such an analysis of national policies affecting teacher quality, working conditions, and professional learning opportunities. In addition, we provide baseline comparisons of teacher qualification, workload and assignments, and collaboration opportunities across a broad range of nations. Our analysis is a blend of analyses of large-scale international survey data from the Trends in International Mathematics and Science Study (TIMSS) with reviews of relevant policy documents as well as in-depth case studies in three nations: the United States, Japan, and Australia. We chose Japan and Australia as both nations produced higher national levels of student achievement than did the United States and have implemented very different approaches to improving teacher quality. We specifically compare the differences and similarities in policies on teacher recruitment, hiring, distribution, professional development, and working conditions in the United States, Australia, and Japan. In addition, the TIMSS 2003 teacher survey provides baseline data from 12 other countries that achieved higher than the United States in the mathematics assessment.

This unique combination of data and analysis provides a global perspective on national educational policies and is quite different from most of the rest of the literature on teacher quality. Previous qualitative comparative studies tended to focus on one or two countries or were reported in edited volumes that combined the perspectives of the authors, with each writing about his or her own nation. Case studies are useful for understanding the lived experiences and cultural perceptions of teachers as well as the impact of the policy contexts they work in, but are difficult to use as a basis for national-level policy recommendations. Large-scale databases can uncover important statistical relationships and highlight differences in national conditions and trends, but typically lack an analysis of national policy contexts and cultural meaning. For that reason, they often lead to misinterpretations of statistical findings and have limited use in creating policy recommendations. By combining both methods, we can overcome the limitations of a single-method study.

In addition, the book explicitly focuses on national policies that affect the entire teaching force in key areas such as recruitment, hiring, and distribution; working conditions; and professional development. The inclusion of specific policy analysis provides a systemic perspective on possible ways to align existing policies with proposed reforms or new policies. This book is unique as a policy study because it shows not only "what should be done" to improve teacher quality based on empirical research, but also "what can be done" based on policy analysis and culturally sensitive case studies. Policy studies often lack reference to approaches to the teacher workforce successful in other nations, so there is often a disconnect between what research suggests and what policies are politically viable. This study addresses the difficult question of "what can be done" in the United States through an analysis of actual policies implemented at

the national level in Australia and Japan. We offer specific recommendations on how U.S. policies should be improved based on empirical evidence
from actual implementation abroad.

WHY AMERICA NEEDS A GLOBAL PERSPECTIVE ON TEACHER QUALITY

Many believe that No Child Left Behind is a uniquely American attempt
at reform—it is not. For nearly 2 decades, the nations of the world have
been affected by transnational forces that have directly influenced national
educational policy. The concern with teacher quality, as we will discuss in
Chapter 1, is virtually worldwide and is part of a much broader concern
with accountability in public education, the institutionalization of human
capital development models, and the increasing influence of multinational
testing (e.g., TIMSS) on national policy making. However, U.S. policy con-
tinues to be made without fully exploiting the range of comparative data
available. For example, the standards-based reforms under NCLB cannot
succeed unless a systemic approach is taken to improve teachers' working
conditions and professional learning opportunities. Ensuring student access to high-quality teachers is major driver of improving student learning, but the current U.S. system does not support the development of a
high-quality teaching workforce through national policies in the way other
nations do. Part of this derives from the decentralized nature of the U.S.
educational system, but there are policy solutions that can overcome the
fragmented approach to recruitment, hiring, professional development,
and working conditions typical in the United States.

More to the point, U.S. policymakers rarely have considered the teaching force from a national, long-term perspective. Comparisons with Japan
and Australia show that U.S. teachers' working conditions—especially the
teaching load and out-of-field teaching responsibilities—are major impediments to achieving high-quality teaching. In addition, U.S. teachers' opportunities to learn are not sustained, do not involve observing peers'
classroom instruction, and are not aligned with teachers' learning needs.
Cross-national comparisons, however, also highlight the strengths of the
U.S. system: its systemic collection of teacher data, its active research community, and the work of national teacher professional associations such
as the National Board for Professional Teaching Standards (NBPTS) and
the Interstate New Teacher Assessment and Support Consortium (INTASC).
All of these are national assets, which are looked upon favorably by other
countries, that U.S. policymakers can use to build coherent and coordinated policies for the teaching force.

To improve the quality of the teacher workforce, federal and state departments of education need to take leadership in aligning teacher policies on recruiting, hiring, and distributing, and continuously supporting teachers based on a shared national vision of high-quality teachers. Professional standards on teacher knowledge, skills, and disposition need to be agreed upon and shared among key stakeholders, including federal and state departments of education, teacher education institutions, teacher unions, superintendents and school board members, professional development providers, school administrators, parents and community members, and most important, teachers. If all stakeholders share the common goals exemplified in teacher professional standards and are given opportunities to discuss implementation processes, they can work to align teacher policies at the federal, state, and local levels to develop and support a high-quality teacher workforce.

GOALS AND ORGANIZATION OF THE BOOK

This book is for anyone who is concerned with the future of U.S. education. It sends clear messages on how U.S. teacher policy needs to be improved so that all students are taught by qualified teachers. Policymakers and administrators should find the messages based on the research data convincing, and teachers will understand how their working conditions and learning opportunities can be improved based on the comparisons with teachers in other countries. Educational researchers will find that this book attempts to move the field of comparative education and educational policy forward to make direct contributions to national policy formation.

The book begins by summarizing the debates on teacher policy and teacher quality. In Chapter 1 the conceptual framework on coherent teacher policy is introduced, and the methods used for the study are explained. In Chapter 2, we present the policy contexts for improving teacher quality in the United States, Australia, and Japan. We compare the national contexts of the three countries and discuss how major federal and national policies are influenced by global trends toward standardization and accountability. The major teacher policies in the three countries are compared and discussed in detail. Then a vision of "high-quality" teachers is presented based on the examination of core statements in professional teacher standards or government documents.

Chapter 3 first discusses the importance, in educational reform, of investing in teacher quality based on empirical evidence on how teacher quality leads to improved student achievement in the United States and cross-nationally. We present comparative data on common features of teacher qualification among the three countries—full certification, subject major, and teaching experience. The national level of teacher qualification, as well as differences in teacher qualification between high-SES (socioeconomic status) schools and low-SES schools, is compared and discussed. Then policies and processes concerning teacher recruitment, hiring, and distribution in Australia and Japan are reviewed and contrasted with those in the United States, and recommendations for systematizing U.S. recruitment and hiring processes, with state leadership, are offered.

Chapter 4 compares two aspects of teachers' working conditions: (1) workload and assignment (instructional workload, multiple-subject teaching assignment, out-of-field teaching, and noninstructional workload) and (2) compensation and benefits (salary, allowance, and leave). Teachers' working conditions are discussed in light of each country's cultural expectations and the role of teachers. State and national policy on teacher allowance and leave in Australia and Japan are examined further. The chapter concludes with recommendations for improving working conditions of U.S. teachers.

In Chapter 5, we first compare national or state policies on teacher induction, mentoring, and professional development in the three countries. We then compare national statistics on the amount and participation rates of mentoring, induction, and professional development activities or programs offered to teachers. To further investigate teacher learning opportunities, we compare the frequency of four types of teacher collaboration: (1) discussions about how to teach a particular concept, (2) preparation of instructional materials, (3) visits to another teacher's classroom to observe his or her teaching, and (4) informal observations of one's own classroom by another teacher. The findings are interpreted in light of cultural and organizational contexts in each country.

We conclude the book in Chapter 6 with summaries of lessons learned from the comparisons of teacher policies on teacher quality, working conditions, and professional learning opportunities in the United States, Australia, and Japan, and a discussion of the policy coherence in these countries. The directions for improving U.S. teacher policy are discussed based on the comparative analyses, and specific recommendations are made on how to improve Title II of NCLB. We conclude with action plans for developing a coherent policy to improve the quality of the U.S. teacher workforce.

Seeking the "Silver Bullet": International Educational Competition and Teacher Quality

IMAGINE A BUSTLING bookstore in a large public university. New titles in education are displayed prominently in the window. All of them concern, in one way or another, a recent international test whose results indicate an astonishingly poor showing among the nation's youth. There are books by respected researchers that offer critiques from both the political right and left. Inside the store, sprinkled among volumes on education and sociology, are "do-it-yourself" guides on education, geared toward anxious parents. Once a nation that prided itself on the educational achievement of its children, this country now endures a daily media barrage of facts and figures that demonstrate the sad state of education and the public schools. This country's schools, the bookstore shopper would conclude, are in serious need of reform.

Most American readers, by now, would have concluded that the country was the United States in the 1990s when the TIMSS provoked a wave of educational debates. They would be wrong. This scene comes from Germany some months after the release of the Programme for International Student Assessment (PISA) in 2003. The PISA data showed that German students had done very poorly compared with their Organisation for Economic Co-operation and Development (OECD) partners (see Steiner-Khamsi, 2004). The German people, once proud of what they considered one of the best educational systems that Europe produced, now found themselves in the low end of the international "horse rankings." (Some of the works on PISA by German authors include Breitsameter, Kissner, & Kordt, 2004; Prenzel, Baumert, & Blum, 2005; Struck, 2008.)

Nations no longer have the freedom to formulate their educational policies in isolation. The rise, rapid expansion, and institutionalization of cross-national educational tests (e.g., TIMSS, PISA, and Progress in International Reading Literacy Study [PIRLS]) have created educational competition that affects all nations (Baker & LeTendre, 2005; Lauder, Brown,

Dillabough, & Halsey, 2006; Tatto, 2007). While everyone is aware of how international economic competition, free-trade zones, and global exchanges have dramatically altered the nature of the world we live in, we rarely think about public schooling as affected by global trends. National policymakers and legislators once considered international studies of education as exotic and often irrelevant. Now, these cross-national studies of school achievement have become common, even mandatory in the sense that more and more nations feel compelled to participate in order to "benchmark" their educational achievements against other nations.

To understand the current problems and trends in the United States—especially the intense focus on teacher quality (variously equated with professional standards, teacher education, certification, quality of instruction, and professional development)—we must understand what has become of our world and our nation's place in it (see Baker & LeTendre, 2005). Educational policy is no longer simply a matter left to each country to do as it will—global trends and pressures affect schooling at every level (Suárez-Orozco & Qin-Hilliard, 2004). The very institutional environment of schools has changed over the past 20 years, and international comparisons have penetrated to the local level. It is no longer uncommon for individual U.S. states, and even some larger school districts, to benchmark to international standards. This new environment drives our attention and our energies, pushing state and federal educational policies in new and unforeseen directions. If we are to successfully plan for the future and effectively reform our educational system, we must understand the global institutional environment. If we wish to truly become more effective at recognizing and improving teacher quality, we must come to terms with the transnational forces at play and understand the interactions between the global culture and national or local cultures that lead to significant differences in national systems and policies for improving the quality of the teaching workforce (Akiba, LeTendre, & Scribner, 2007; Anderson-Levitt, 2003; Baker & LeTendre, 2005; LeTendre, Baker, Akiba, Goesling, & Wiseman, 2001a).

THE GLOBAL MOVEMENT TO IMPROVE TEACHER CREDENTIALS AND QUALITY

We are now in the midst of a massive global movement to upgrade teacher credentials, revamp teacher education, and thereby improve the quality of instruction and of education (OECD, 2004, 2005; UNESCO Institute for Statistics, 2006). The inclusion of teacher credential provisions in NCLB and the creation of teacher professional standards by the INTASC and

NBPTS to identify "qualified" teachers are not uniquely American phenomena. Although the extremely decentralized nature of the U.S. educational system has given an added imperative to the standardization movement, the United States appears to be caught up in the same type of policy debates and reform initiatives as the rest of the world.

Some might argue that these concerns are simply an outgrowth of the political attacks mounted in the 1990s on public education and teacher training programs. Indeed, the publication of books bashing teacher education programs, as well as schools or colleges of education in general, became a small industry in the late 1990s (Berliner & Biddle, 1995; Kramer, 1991; Labaree, 2004). Many books, often with a conservative political agenda, argued that education schools basically provided teachers in training with idealistic notions and outdated theories. After *A Nation at Risk* was published in 1983 (National Commission on Excellence in Education, 1983), some prominent teacher education scholars argued that international studies were being used deliberately to create a "myth" of educational crisis (Berliner & Biddle, 1995). Reports like Walberg (1998) and the Fordham Foundation (1999)—critical of existing institutions of teacher education and certification—sounded a surprising call from the political right for more (and better) teachers. As Lora Cohen-Vogel noted, there has been a long-term increase in the federal role in teacher preparation and professional development. She argues that beginning with the Sputnik scare of the 1950s (National Defense Education Act of 1958), the power to influence teacher preparation has increased at the federal level, but that systematic alignment of policy goals remains an issue.

By the mid-1990s, there was already a significant literature on the global state of dissatisfaction with teacher education (Grossman & McDonald, 2008; Steiner-Khamsi, 1999). What might appear to be an American shift from a focus on curriculum to a focus on instruction—mobilized in part by a conservative political agenda to weaken public schools—actually looks more like a very large global trend to focus on human capital development. The focus of the debates of the 1980s and 1990s has shifted from institutionalizing a core curriculum to providing high-quality instruction and highly trained instructors. More recent scholarship focuses on the lack of leadership training and principals' role in improving teacher quality (Monk, 2008), further broadening the debate about how to reform teacher training programs. Policies focusing on teacher certification, instructional quality and its monitoring (i.e., various formulations of opportunity to learn [OTL]), and/or school quality draw on a core logic that to improve education and to compete economically, states have to recruit, train, and retain a highly talented workforce of teachers. States like Arizona, Kansas, and North Carolina show increasing willingness to spend tax dollars measuring, monitoring, and (hopefully) improving the quality of instruction that teachers provide (see www.aztwc.org, www.kantell.org, and www.ncptsc.org, respectively).

Many have pointed to the passage of No Child Left Behind in 2002 as the driving force behind states' activities to control teacher quality. At a national level, NCLB did indeed create pressure on states to meet the standard of providing a highly qualified teacher in every classroom. NCLB does appear to be part of an ongoing "accountability movement" in educational reform. Major organizational actors (such as the Council of Chief State School Officers) readily weighed in on the debate and created national standards for teacher quality and certification (Blank, 2003), although the effect on practice was not always clearly in the direction indicated by policy (Smith, Desimone, & Ueno, 2005). However, we argue that the United States is but one case of many around the globe where nations underwent significant policy reform with regard to teacher training, quality, and certification. The current obsession with teacher education, credentials, and quality is not driven by NCLB or a politically motivated "accountability" movement (Ota, 2000). Rather, it is part of a global trend in which national policymakers, educational researchers, and scholars exhibit concern with the teacher workforce as a key element in national economic competition.

While these concerns are not necessarily new, the emphasis on teachers as a workforce that needs to be managed at the national level—similar to the way that nations attempt to manage the workforce in areas like science and technology—is new, and it raises significant questions that go well beyond the old debates about what the public schools should do in order to maintain America's economic competitiveness. The current drive to understand what affects teacher quality represents a transnational acceptance of the logic of human capital development and an acceptance of a direct link between educational achievement and national economic potential. The former provides a cogent rationale for improving teacher training, support in the workplace, and professional development, while the latter provides powerful political capital to mobilize resources and enact policy or legislation.

The institutionalization of these twin themes in international educational and developmental dialogues has altered substantially the way that the United States and all other nations operate public education. In the past, we and our colleagues have been critical of the impact that cross-national comparisons can have on policy (LeTendre & Akiba, 2000), and of the unquestioning acceptance of the logic that equates more and better education with a stronger and more resilient economy (Baker & LeTendre, 2005). But international tests have now attained the kind of legitimacy once reserved for national assessments, and cross-national benchmarking is now an accepted part of how nations evaluate their school systems. Rather than try to resist these trends, we argue that policymakers need to understand how these forces constrain national policy, and learn from cross-national comparative studies that examine how various countries develop and implement teacher policy differently.

There is increasing global pressure on all nations to institute and enact standards and monitor the teaching force in ways more similar to the management of national health care or national defense systems. This pressure can be seen either as a threat to national autonomy or as an opportunity to improve teachers' working conditions and the quality of instruction our children receive in public school. Carefully conducted cross-national comparisons can allow policymakers to identify important elements of the best recruitment or professional development models. Multiple international reports on teacher quality by the OECD (2004, 2005) and UNESCO (UNESCO Institute for Statistics, 2006) have focused on teacher certification and subject training as measures of teacher quality. The training, certification, and periodic assessment of teachers to promote educational quality have become a global priority and the object of considerable political attention around the world. As a nation, we now have a unique opportunity to assess our national teaching force and identify changes that would best serve our students and teachers.

TEACHER QUALITY AROUND THE WORLD

The United States is one of many countries that began to institute reforms aimed at higher standards and increased certification for teachers during the past 10 years (Steiner-Khamsi, 2004; Moon, 2007). In the United States, the focus on certification has been informed by research on "out-of-field" teaching (Ingersoll, 1999, 2001) as well as by comparative and international studies that identified weaknesses in instructional practices and environments surrounding U.S. teachers in comparison with those in high-achieving countries (Hiebert et al., 2005; Stigler & Hiebert, 1999). Policymakers and academics alike looked to international data to benchmark U.S. performance, often trying to identify "best practices" among teachers in high-scoring countries.

Education policymakers around the world have come to recognize teacher quality as a major vehicle by which to improve student learning (OECD, 2004, 2005; UNESCO Institute for Statistics, 2006). Attracting competent candidates to the teaching profession, retaining highly qualified teachers by providing support and incentives, and ensuring students' access to high-quality teaching have been central issues in educational reforms in many countries. According to a study of 25 countries conducted from 2002 to 2004 (OECD, 2005), policymakers in the majority of those countries were struggling with the problems resulting from a lack of highly qualified teachers, especially in science- and math-related subjects; the low social status and salary of teachers and their poor working conditions; a lack of systemic induction programs; and inequitable distribution of qualified teachers between high-poverty and low-poverty schools. UNESCO (UNESCO Institute for Statistics, 2006) also reports a severe teacher shortage in sub-Saharan African countries, the Arab States, and South Asian countries. Many countries around the world share the same concerns about teacher quality as U.S. policymakers and administrators.

Previous international studies also laid the groundwork for the comparison of teacher quality. These studies demonstrated that mathematics teachers in high-achieving countries tended to demonstrate balanced attention to challenging content, procedural skills, and conceptual understanding, whereas U.S. teachers' instructional practice was characterized by a focus on lower level mathematics skills (Hiebert et al., 2005). Our own study on teacher work roles revealed that U.S. mathematics teachers were assigned to teach multiple subjects and multiple grade levels more often than were Japanese mathematics teachers, who usually taught only mathematics and only one grade level (LeTendre et al., 2001a).

To date, international studies of teacher quality have focused on teacher education and certification, not on teachers' work roles, professional development, or the institutional environment (Ingersoll, 2007; Wang, Coleman, Coley, & Phelps, 2003). For example, a study conducted by the Educational Testing Service compared the United States with high-achieving countries—Australia, England, Hong Kong, Japan, Korea, the Netherlands, and Singapore—in eighth-grade mathematics and science teacher education and development policies (Wang et al., 2003). This study found that all the countries except the United States and Australia had centralized systems of teacher education and certification with tight regulatory control by the central government. All of the high-achieving countries had screening at multiple points—entry to teacher education program, evaluation of field experience, exit from teacher education program, or certification—whereas in the United States teacher licensure testing was the only major high-stakes criterion for determining who became a teacher. Furthermore, induction programs for new teachers were required in England, Singapore, Japan, and most states in Australia, but in the United States induction programs were fragmented because of the variations in policies and resources available.

Most recently, McKinsey & Company (2007) examined the 11 highest achieving systems in the PISA 2003 assessment (Alberta, Australia, Belgium, Finland, Hong Kong, Japan, the Netherlands, New Zealand, Ontario, Singapore, and South Korea) to identify what high-performing school systems have in common. They identified three characteristics of high-achieving countries:

1. Getting the right people to become teachers
2. Developing them into effective instructors
3. Ensuring that the system is able to deliver the best possible instruction for every child.

In these countries, the top one third of college students in academic standing are recruited into teacher education programs using selective entry requirements; once they begin teaching, they are provided with high-quality mentoring and professional development programs to continuously improve instruction, along with a competitive salary. Students also are ensured access to high-quality instruction through the government's allocation of additional funds and support to low-performing schools. McKinsey & Company have argued that applying these best practices universally could improve failing school systems regardless of their location.

The importance of investing in improving teacher quality also was empirically shown in our most recent analyses of 46 countries, using TIMSS 2003 data (Akiba et al., 2007). We found that the countries with a greater percentage of qualified mathematics teachers—teachers with full certification, subject major, and 3 or more years of teaching experience—produced significantly higher national mathematics achievement, after controlling for gross domestic product (GDP) per capita and educational expenditure as a percentage of GDP. The study also found that while the national level of teacher quality in the United States was about the international average, the "opportunity gap" in students' access to highly qualified teachers between wealthy and poor students was the fourth largest of the 39 countries.

DEVELOPING A COHERENT POLICY
FOR IMPROVING TEACHER QUALITY

These previous studies provide a basis for identifying characteristics of successful policies and practices supporting teacher quality. A successful system for teachers attracts the most academically able candidates into teaching, provides high-quality teacher training, and continuously supports them through attractive working conditions and high-quality induction and professional development programs. Most important, the system is coherently structured to support teachers in continuously improving themselves toward becoming high-quality teachers, and is supported by multiple stakeholders across national, state, and local levels. Based on the emerging characteristics of a successful system for improving teacher quality, we have developed the conceptual framework for a coherent policy shown in Figure 1.1.

If we are to systemically improve the quality of the U.S. teaching workforce, we need a system that simultaneously addresses multiple processes for developing a high-quality workforce based on the vision of the characteristics of high-quality teachers shared among national, state, and local stakeholders. In the United States, multiple agencies, including teacher education institutions, school districts, state departments of education, and professional development providers, implement the policies and practices for recruiting and training teacher candidates, hiring and distributing qualified teachers, and continuously supporting and retaining teachers. Unless these multiple agencies agree on a shared vision of high-quality teachers and coordinate the roles for developing and promoting the characteristics of high-quality teachers—in other words, unless they have a common goal—the system is likely to fail to produce expected outcomes.

A country's teacher professional standards can serve as this common goal. In the United States, there is general professional consensus on the teacher standards created by the INTASC and NBPTS, which have been modeled by the teacher professional standards in many states (Interstate New Teacher Assessment and Support Consortium, 1992; National Board for Professional Teaching Standards, 1994). However, the vision of high-quality teachers in these standards is not reflected in the "highly qualified" teacher requirements in No Child Left Behind. This creates an

Figure 1.1. Conceptual model of a coherent teacher policy.

inconsistency of goals in policies on recruitment, hiring, and professional support. The nature of NCLB in comparison with major teacher policies in Australia and Japan is examined carefully in Chapter 2.

In recruitment and training processes, the most academically able candidates who are committed to teaching need to be recruited into teacher education programs, and they need to be provided with high-quality training that integrates theory and practice with extended internship experiences under coherent goals. Rigorous criteria based on the teacher professional standards need to be applied at the point of entry into training and at the certification stage to select only the most qualified candidates. In the United States, only 42% of new recipients of bachelor of education degrees were teaching 1 year later (Ingersoll, 2003a), which shows a large group of certified candidates choosing not to seek employment as teachers. When rigorous criteria combined with strong financial and professional incentives are used to select the most qualified and committed candidates both at the entry to teacher training and at the certification stage, the status of teaching will likely shift from a backup plan to a lifelong profession.

In hiring and distribution processes, rigorous selection criteria based on the teacher professional standards need to be used to hire the most qualified candidates into teaching. A major problem in the United States is the unequal distribution of qualified teachers between wealthy suburban schools and inner-city, high-poverty schools (Akiba et al., 2007; Ascher & Fruchter, 2001; Darling-Hammond, 2004; Jerald & Ingersoll, 2002; Peske & Haycock, 2006; Shen, Mansberger, & Yang, 2004). To distribute qualified teachers equally across schools, thereby ensuring every student's access to high-quality teachers, strong incentive programs are needed to attract high-quality teachers into inner-city, high-poverty schools. Financial support from federal and state departments of education to school districts serving these schools is a critical component of the effort to equalize student access to high-quality teachers.

In the processes of continuously supporting and retaining high-quality teachers, it is important to maintain attractive working conditions and provide high-quality teacher induction and professional development programs. Working conditions, including salary, teaching load, out-of-field teaching, and noninstructional duties, are important factors that encourage or discourage teachers to stay in teaching. All new teachers have to be provided with an induction or mentoring program for the smooth transition from teacher education programs to a complex school setting with multiple responsibilities. A reduced workload for new teachers is critical so that they can learn to develop their teaching methods based on student background, community, and school culture. Teachers need continuous support for participating in professional development throughout their careers so that they can gain up-to-date knowledge and skills and maintain high standards of teaching as a "learning profession" (Darling-Hammond & Sykes, 1999).

These processes of recruitment and training, hiring and distribution, and continuously supporting and retaining teachers are interdependent on one another and cannot exist in isolation. For example, unless teachers are provided with attractive working conditions and continuous learning opportunities, it is not possible to attract the most academically successful students into teacher education programs and the teaching profession. Successful recruitment also depends on the incentives offered in the hiring process. Likewise, the distribution process cannot succeed unless teachers are provided with strong financial incentives and improved working conditions in hard-to-staff schools, as well as both enhanced learning opportunities useful for teaching in diverse, inner-city schools and reduced teaching load. All of these processes influence the capacity of the teaching profession to retain high-quality teachers.

Finally, this multiple-process, coherent policy for improving teacher quality cannot be successfully implemented unless it is supported by all key stakeholders, which include federal and state departments of education, teacher education institutions, teacher unions, school districts, school administrators, parents, and most important, teachers. Collaboration and coordination among these key stakeholders are critical for developing a coherent policy and designating and reassessing roles that make sense to all. The coherent policy becomes successful when teachers can see clearly how the processes of recruitment and training, hiring and distribution, and professional support are aligned to support them in developing into high-quality teachers, and when they truly value this support system as a driving force for improving the teaching profession and student learning opportunities.

The importance of congruence or coherence in policy for the success of education reforms has been pointed out many times during the past decade (Cohen & Hill, 2001; Darling-Hammond & Sykes, 2003; National Commission on Teaching and America's Future, 1996; Wilson, Darling-Hammond, & Berry, 2001). The importance of improving working conditions and professional learning opportunities also has been argued in these reports. Some of these reports introduced successful cases of state- and district-level implementation of standards-based reforms that were coherent and that provided high-quality professional development programs and extra support to hard-to-staff schools to improve working conditions, yet such success was limited to a small number of states and districts (Darling-Hammond & Sykes, 2003; Wilson, Darling-Hammond, & Berry, 2001).

The decentralized educational system in the United States is characterized by the role of federal and state governments, which set the goals through legislations but leave the implementation processes for achieving the goals to local districts and schools. For example, Title II of NCLB set the goal of every teacher meeting the "highly qualified" guideline, and each state department of education specified the criteria for highly-qualified teachers and has been reporting the percentage of highly-qualified teachers at the school and district level. How to staff schools with highly qualified teachers is left to local districts and schools, which are held accountable for achieving the goals set by the federal and state departments of education. This distribution of power among multilevel governance structures without a coordinated sense-making process for the policy or reform goals often leads to a fragmented implementation of a new policy (Fuhrman, Goertz, & Weinbaum, 2007).

Studies of district and school responses to federal and state policies have shown that districts and schools interpret a new policy in ways that allow it to be accommodated within existing structure and culture, intentionally or unintentionally, and often fail to reflect the original goals (Spillane, 2004). District and school resources and capacities and community and teacher responses influence the sense-making and decision-making processes for implementing a new policy (Coburn, 2006; Sipple, Killeen, & Monk, 2004). What is critically needed is the opportunity to collectively identify problems, establish a goal, and specify implementation processes among key stakeholders to develop a coherent policy for improving teacher quality.

To scale up a coherent policy for improving teacher quality to the national level in the United States, it is important to look into successful national cases. This comparative study illustrates how two countries— Australia and Japan—have developed or are in the process of developing a coherent policy for improving teacher quality. Both countries have focused their national policies on teacher quality and have taken a systemic approach to improving the quality of the teaching workforce. Australia takes systemic approaches to recruitment, hiring, and distribution to ensure a sufficient supply of qualified teachers and equalize student access to them. The use of state or territory databases to match candidates to open positions, and strong incentive packages offered to those who teach in hard-to-staff schools in rural and remote areas and in subject areas of teacher shortage (e.g., math, science), achieved more equal distribution of qualified teachers across each state or territory than exists in the United States.

Japan has a centralized system for offering induction, mentoring, and professional development opportunities in collaboration with teacher educators and teacher leaders. Professional learning is well integrated into teachers' responsibilities and daily schedules, and learning opportunities are structured with both on-site and off-site activities along the continuum of professional development stages. A strong culture and organizational support of teacher collaboration for instructional improvement, offered through Lesson Study—in which teachers collaboratively plan, observe, and discuss lessons—bolster teachers' learning opportunities as well. These policies and cultural and organizational supports led to a greater amount of time devoted to professional learning among Japanese teachers than U.S. or Australian teachers.

While these two countries provide successful cases in some of the processes depicted in Figure 1.1, neither country excels in all the processes or in the alignment of the processes. This book carefully examines the struggles and challenges faced by both countries in their attempts to establish a system for improving the overall quality of the teaching workforce, and there are important lessons to be learned from these experiences for U.S. policymakers and practitioners. The comparisons among the three countries also shed light on the strengths in U.S. policies and practices, strengths that often are revealed in Australia's and Japan's efforts to follow or emulate U.S. policies or practices. Those strengths are advanced national- and state-level database systems on teachers and their environments—which have a great potential for research-based policy development and implementation—and the capacity of professional organizations, such as the INTASC, the NBPTS, and the National Council for Accreditation of Teacher Education (NCATE), to develop high-quality professional standards, assessment or advanced certification processes, and teacher education program accreditation.

Thus, this cross-national comparison among the three countries not only offers opportunities to learn from the successes and challenges experienced by Australia and Japan, but also reassesses the strengths of the U.S. system that we can build on in promoting teacher quality reforms. In Chapters 2 through 5, policies and practices on teacher recruitment, hiring, distribution, working conditions, and professional learning opportunities are carefully examined and interpreted in each cultural and national context, and recommendations for U.S. policy are offered. Although there have been many comparative studies on teacher quality in the past, most have focused on teacher education or certification (Akiba et al., 2007; Schmidt et al., 2007; Wang et al., 2003). No previous study has taken a systemic approach to examining how teacher policy impacts teacher quality; thus this book creates a new knowledge base from which U.S. policymakers can develop a coherent teacher policy on teacher recruitment and hiring, working conditions, and professional learning opportunities.

Applying a mixed-methods approach to teacher survey data, policy documents, and case studies, we address the following questions:

1. How does teacher quality measured from multiple dimensions (e.g., certification, subject major, teaching experience) in the United States differ from that in Australia and Japan, and how do the policies on teacher recruitment, hiring, and distribution explain the difference?
2. How do working conditions of U.S. teachers differ from those of Australian and Japanese teachers, and what policies and systems explain the difference?
3. How do U.S. teachers' opportunities for professional learning differ from those in Australia and Japan, and what policies and structures for teacher induction and professional development exist in the three countries?
4. What lessons can we learn from the comparison of teacher policies in the three countries, and what U.S. policies offer promise for successfully improving teacher quality?

RESEARCH METHODS

We have examined the status of teacher quality, working conditions, and professional learning opportunities in the United States in comparison with high-achieving countries using teacher survey data in TIMSS collected during 2003. The TIMSS data were collected from eighth-grade mathematics teachers in a nationally representative sample of schools in 46 countries, including 340 U.S. teachers, 197 Australian teachers, and 146 Japanese teachers. This data set provides the most extensive data currently available in international data sets, including PISA and PIRL, on teacher quality, working conditions, and professional learning opportunities.

The TIMSS 2003 data allowed us to compare teacher quality and contextualize the U.S. teaching workforce globally through comparisons with Australia, Japan, and 12 other countries that achieved higher than the United States (Belgium [Flemish], Estonia, Hong Kong, Hungary, Latvia, Malaysia, the Netherlands, the Russian Federation, Singapore, the Slovak Republic, South Korea, and Taiwan). In addition, we supplemented the TIMSS 2003 data with international data from the OECD and UNESCO. The chapters of this book provide details of the TIMSS teacher survey questions and response choices from which the data were drawn, as well as data analysis methods.

Extensive policy document analyses were conducted to understand the nature of teacher policies on recruitment, hiring and distribution, and professional support through improving working conditions and professional learning opportunities. The policy documents initially were collected through the Web sites of federal and state departments of education, and we corresponded extensively by e-mail with federal and state representatives to confirm the accuracy of our understanding of the policies, legislation, regulations, and standards in each country, and to gather missing documentation. We spent about a year (2007) gathering all the documents needed for our study.

To further understand the background, history, and processes of major teacher policy, we also visited Japan and Australia during 2008. In Japan, we interviewed officers in the Ministry of Education, Culture, Sports, Science and Technology; the Education Policy Research Center under that Ministry; and prefecture and local boards of education. We also interviewed several teachers to understand their perspectives on the major teacher policies. In Australia, we interviewed a coordinator of the Australian Government Quality Teacher Programme in the New South Wales Department of Education and Training, Australian Education Union representatives in Victoria, representatives of the New South Wales Institute of Teachers and the Victoria Institute of Teaching (teacher registration and teacher program accreditation bodies), and researchers at the Australian Council for Educational Research. In both Japan and Australia, we communicated with a number of university researchers who are experts in teacher quality and teacher policy.

We further supplemented the TIMSS data and policy document analyses with knowledge and experience from our previous ethnographies, case study, and survey research in Japan and the United States over the past decade (Akiba, 2004, 2008; Akiba et al., 2007; Baker & LeTendre, 2005; Fukuzawa & LeTendre, 2001; LeTendre, 1999, 2000; LeTendre & Akiba, 2001; LeTendre et al., 2001a). The information from our previous work is based on interviews with a number of teachers, school administrators, students, and parents, and on survey data collected from students and teachers in Japan and the United States.

This book is different from previous books comparing education in the United States and other countries because it focuses on how "quality" in teaching is connected to the working life of teachers and school environments. Like Baker and LeTendre (2005), we use both large-scale survey data and rich ethnographic and case studies to shed light on teacher quality in the United States as part of a global cultural context. Cross-national survey data are excellent sources for placing U.S. teacher and educational practices along a broad international continuum. Ethnographic and case studies show the details of policy and cultural contexts that determine the role of teachers and impact teacher quality. Both types of data are necessary to make valid comparisons that can generate viable policy and reforms.

We also pay close attention to variation in teacher quality within countries. Previous comparative studies, including our own, typically have focused on cross-national variation and rarely have examined how variation within a country constrains or promotes different practices and reforms. For example, the national level of out-of-field teaching does not tell us how such practice differentially hinders teachers in inner-city, high-poverty schools compared with their peers in wealthy, suburban schools. When we present data on teacher quality, working conditions, and professional learning opportunities, we will show both the national average as well as the difference between wealthy schools and high-poverty schools. Such data bring to light how nations differ in the inequality of students' access to qualified teachers (Akiba et al., 2007).

Finally, our book shows not only the successful cases but also the failures and challenges, which are sometimes the most salient policy lessons. Japanese and Australian policymakers and legislators have been criticized for certain reforms made in an attempt to improve teacher quality. Past comparative studies often presented other countries as ideals that the United States should model itself after and ignored the contested (and occasionally disastrous) policies such nations instituted. It is important to know that all high-achieving countries have experienced both successes and failures, and the most valuable lessons for improving teacher quality in the United States come from understanding the entire experience—both positive and negative aspects—in other countries' efforts to reform teacher quality.

We argue that standards-based reforms under NCLB will not succeed unless a systemic approach is taken to improving teachers' working conditions and professional learning opportunities. Ensuring student access to high-quality teachers is a major driver of improving student learning, and the current U.S. system does not support the development of a high-quality teaching workforce because of the fragmented approach to recruitment, hiring, professional development, and working conditions. Comparisons with Japan and Australia show that U.S. teachers' working conditions—especially teaching load and out-of-field teaching responsibilities—are major impediments to achieving high-quality teaching. In addition, U.S. teachers' opportunities to learn are not sustained, do not involve observing peers' classroom instruction, and are not aligned with teachers' learning needs. Cross-national comparisons, however, also show the strengths of the United States, which include systemic teacher data management at national and state levels and national accreditation bodies for teacher education programs. These strengths are looked up to by other countries, and the United States can build upon them in its development of a coherent teacher policy.

To improve the quality of the teacher workforce, federal and state departments of education need to take leadership in aligning teacher policies on recruiting, hiring and distributing, and continuously supporting teachers based on the vision of high-quality teachers. As pointed out earlier, teacher professional standards on teacher knowledge, skills, and disposition need to be agreed upon and shared among all key stakeholders, including federal and state departments of education, teacher education institutions, teacher unions, superintendents and school board members, professional development providers, school administrators, parents and community members, and most important, teachers. When all stakeholders share the common goals exemplified in teacher professional standards, they can work concertedly to align teacher policies at federal, state, and local levels to develop and support a high-quality teacher workforce.

CHAPTER 2

Policy Contexts in the United States, Australia, and Japan

IN THIS CHAPTER, we begin by providing some background information and introducing the national policy contexts of three countries—the United States, Australia, and Japan. We compare teacher and student populations, economic standing, educational expenditure, education governance structures and public school funding, and international assessment results in mathematics and science. Next, we describe characteristics of major educational reforms in each country and major trends in teacher-related reforms to explicate the policy contexts. Major teacher policies and reforms in each country are introduced and discussed. We will show how major educational reforms are influenced by the global trend toward standardization and accountability. Finally, we compare teachers' roles in these three countries based on an analysis of teacher professional standards or guidelines that depict a vision of high-quality teachers. By examining the policy and cultural contexts in the United States, Australia, and Japan, this chapter sets the stage for the in-depth analyses of teacher quality and teacher-related policies provided in Chapters 3 through 5.

COMPARISON OF NATIONAL CONTEXTS IN THE UNITED STATES, AUSTRALIA, AND JAPAN

Before discussing national policy and reforms related to teachers in the United States, Australia, and Japan, it is important to understand the national contexts in these countries. National political and cultural contexts play an important role in defining the type of policies that can be implemented, as well as how the nation may respond to global forces.

Table 2.1 presents background statistics for the three countries, gathered from various sources. Beginning with the most basic statistic, population, we can already see that U.S. policymakers must deal with a system that dwarfs its Japanese and Australian counterparts in terms of number of teachers and students in elementary and secondary schools. The United

Table 2.1. Comparison of national contexts and background information.

	United States	Australia	Japan
Population [a]	302,841,000	20,000,000	127,953,000
Number of Teachers (Elementary & Secondary)	3,588,000 [b] (87% public)	235,795 [c] (66% public)	856,379 [d] (92% public)
Number of Students (Elementary & Secondary)	54,928,000 [b] (89% public)	3,348,139 [c] (67% public)	14,429,115 [d] (90% public)
% of language minority [e]	16.6%	20.2%	5.8%
GDP per capita [a]	US$41,890	US$31,794	US$31,267
Education expenditure as % of GDP [a]	5.3	4.5	3.5
Units of Education Governance	Federal 50 states/DC School districts	Commonwealth 6 states/2 territories Regions	National 47 prefectures/ 51 major cities Cities and towns
Public School Funding	Federal: 9.1% [f] State: 47.1% District: 43.9%	Commonwealth: 22%[g] State/Territories: 78%	National: 33% [h] Prefecture: 67%
TIMSS 2003 Mathematics Eighth graders [i]	504	505	570
TIMSS 2003 Science Eighth graders [i]	527	527	552
PISA 2006 Math Literacy 15-year-olds [j]	474	520	523
PISA 2006 Science Literacy 15-year-olds [j]	489	527	531

[a] UNESCO Institute for Statistics, 2008. (2005 data)

[b] National Center for Educational Statistics, 2007. (2005 data)

[c] Australian Bureau of Statistics, 2006. (2005 data)

[d] Ministry of Education, Culture, Sports, Science and Technology, 2007a. (2005 data)

[e] The percentage of eighth graders who speak a language other than the official language of the country at home based on the student survey data in the TIMSS 2003 data set.

[f] Sable & Hill, 2006. Percentages do not sum to 100 due to rounding.

[g] Dowling, 2007.

[h] Shimizu, Akao, Atai, Ito, Sato, et al., 2006.

[i] TIMSS & PIRLS International Study Center, 2006.

[j] National Center for Education Statistics, 2008a.

States has about 3.6 million teachers compared with 856,000 in Japan and 236,000 in Australia. There are about 55 million students in the United States compared with 14 million in Japan and 3 million in Australia. Like Japan's, the U.S. system is largely a public one: About 90% of teachers and students are in public schools in both nations. In Australia, however, there is a large private sector divided between Catholic schools and independent schools, which together hire 34% of teachers and enroll 33% of students.

We also see significant differences in other basic parameters, but perhaps not in the way that many American readers would imagine. The student population is more linguistically diverse in Australia than in the United States or Japan. According to student survey data in the TIMSS 2003, 20.2% of Australian eighth graders and 16.6% percent of U.S. eighth graders report that they speak a language other than English at home. In Japan, only 5.8% speak a language other than Japanese at home.

Gross domestic product per capita—an indicator of the country's economic wealth—is larger in the United States (US$41,890) than in Australia (US$31,794) and Japan (US$31,267). The United States also invests a larger percentage of GDP in education (5.3%) than does Australia (4.5%) or Japan (3.5%). The units of education governance in the United States are the federal Department of Education, 50 state departments of education, and numerous school districts within each state. In Australia, the Department of Education, Employment and Workplace Relations (DEEWR) serves as the government (commonwealth) education governance unit, and there are six state and two territory departments of education. Within each state or territory, there are multiple regions. Regional offices function as branches of state/territory departments of education, with limited autonomy and decision-making power.

Decentralization is a key element of the national policy contexts in the United States and Australia, where the constitutional right and responsibility of education resides in state governments. In the United States, the state governments have delegated the responsibility to local school districts for most of the country's history (Fuhrman, Goertz, & Weinbaum, 2007). In sharp contrast, the national government in Japan has the constitutional right and responsibility of education. The Ministry of Education serves as the national education governance unit. There are 47 prefecture boards of education, 15 special city boards of education, and 36 central city boards of education. Within each prefecture, there are multiple local boards of education, but all are subordinate to higher levels of administration.

In terms of public school funding, Australia and Japan have similar structures. In contrast to the United States, where the federal government provides only 9.1% of public school funding, in Australia, 22% of public school funding comes from the DEEWR (commonwealth government), and in Japan, 33% comes from the Ministry of Education (national government). The rest of the funding is provided by state/territory departments of education in Australia and prefecture/special city/central city boards of education in Japan. Until 2006, 50% of public school funding was provided by the Ministry in Japan, but the funding was reduced to 33% to promote decentralized education governance (Shimizu et al., 2006).

The United States and Australia had similar national achievement levels in mathematics and science in the Trends in International Mathematics and Science Study (2003 data), but Australia achieved higher than the United States in the Programme for International Student Assessment (2006 data). Japan achieved higher than the United States and Australia in the TIMSS assessments, but Japan's achievement in the PISA assessments was similar to that of Australia. Compared with the TIMSS, the PISA assessments include a greater number of open-ended items that require student writing of solutions to real-life problems, and thus test mathematics and science literacy focused on the application of math and science knowledge in daily practices, which assesses higher order thinking and problem solving. Therefore, while U.S. students did well in multiple-choice items in the TIMSS, their performance in real-life application and problem solving was not as high as that of students in Australia and Japan.

Overall, the U.S. system is much more massive than its Japanese or Australian counterparts, but it is not necessarily more diverse and certainly is as well funded. Given these basic facts (and the overall high GDP for the United States), the low average student scores on some of the major international tests have led some critics to wonder whether the United States is getting less for its educational investment than other nations (see Walberg, 1998). We reject this explanation as overly simplistic, because it does not account for other significant factors, such as within-nation economic inequality. However, we do believe that there may be substantial room for the United States to better allocate educational resources and better coordinate how educational dollars are distributed. U.S. educational reformers must seriously consider the constraints that a massive, highly decentralized system places on U.S. schools.

POLICY CONTEXT: STANDARDIZATION AND ACCOUNTABILITY

Despite the major differences in national contexts across the three countries, educational policy and reforms in these countries have been consistent with larger global trends toward standardization and accountability. In the United States, standardization and accountability have been manifested in No Child Left Behind in the form of requirements that all states establish content standards and implement a state assessment system that tests all students in Grades 3 through 8 and once in high school in mathematics and reading. States, districts, and schools are held accountable for meeting adequate yearly progress (AYP) goals determined by each state. District- and school-level achievement and whether each school has met the AYP goals must be reported to the public. In addition, these results need to be disaggregated by race, gender, English language proficiency, disability, and socioeconomic status.

Districts and schools that fail to meet the AYP goals are identified as "needing improvement." If the schools cannot meet the AYP goals after 2 years, all students need to be offered public school choice. After a school has failed to meet the AYP goals for 3 years, its students are allowed to transfer to a higher performing public or private school or receive supplemental educational services from a provider of their choice. Schools and states that make significant progress in closing the achievement gap will receive awards in the form of a "No Child Left Behind" school bonus fund and an "Achievement in Education" state bonus fund. States that fail to meet AYP goals for their disadvantaged students will risk losing part of their federal funding.

In Australia, there is more movement toward developing a nationally consistent student assessment system (Department of Education, Science and Training [DEST], 2007). Since the 1999 agreement on National Goals for Schooling in the 21st Century (the Adelaide Declaration) adopted by the Ministerial Council on Education, Employment, Training and Youth Affairs (MCEETYA), student achievement based on the National Assessment Program has been reported against agreed benchmarks in core subject areas. Starting with reading assessment in Grades 3 and 5 in 1999, the subjects and grade levels tested have increased to reading, writing, and mathematics in Grades 3, 5, 7, and 9 in 2008 (MCEETYA, 2006). The achievement results are reported by each state, school location (remote, provincial, metropolitan), socioeconomic status, and ethnicity (comparison between indigenous students and nonindigenous students).

The achievement results based on the National Assessment Program, however, are not tied to rewards or sanctions. Instead, to support schools' effort to improve student learning under the Investing in Our Schools Programme, the Australian Government provided A$1.2 billion (the 2004 Australian dollar is equivalent to about 1.2 American dollars) "to fund small-scale projects which improve the infrastructure of schools in accordance with priorities identified by the communities, parents, friends, and teachers associated with each school" (DEST, 2007, p. 50). More than 7,500 school projects—including ones focusing on classroom upgrades, up-to-date computer labs, and safe playgrounds—across the country have been funded to date. In addition, approximately A$2 billion was funded from 2005 to 2008 under the Literacy, Numeracy and Special Learning Needs Programme to support the improvement of the learning outcomes of educationally disadvantaged students, including students with a disability, newly arrived students with English as a Second Language, and geographically isolated students.

Under the School Assistance Act 2004, "Statements of Learning" that describe the knowledge, skills, and understandings and capacities that all Australian students should have the opportunity to learn and develop in five subject areas—English, mathematics, science, civics and citizenship, and information and communications technology (ICT)—were developed during 2005 and 2006 by the National Consistency in Curriculum Outcomes Steering Committee, which consists of state and territory education system officials (MCEETYA, 2008). The Statements were implemented in 2008 in each state and territory by either incorporating them into existing curriculum documents or showing the alignments between them and existing curriculum documents.

Global trends toward greater standardization and accountability also have influenced Japan, which already had a long history of examination systems (Zeng, 1999). For most of the post-World War II era, the results of prefecture-level high school entrance examinations and the national central examination for entrance into higher education were nationally available. The Ministry of Education established the National Achievement and Learning Assessment, and since 2007 all students in Grade 6 (at the end of elementary school) and Grade 9 (at the end of middle school) are assessed in literacy and mathematics annually (Ministry of Education, Culture, Sports, Science and Technology [MEXT], 2007e). Within each grade level and subject, the assessment results are reported by prefecture and school location (remote, town, small city, mid-size city, large city). These assessment results are not reported at the school level and are not tied to rewards or sanctions.

The School Evaluation System was established based on the legislative requirement in Article 42 of School Education Law in 2007 for the purpose of evaluating school management and educational activities (MEXT, 2008a). The System involves both self-evaluation and external evaluation. Since 2002, the Ministry has supported research on external evaluation methods and supported prefecture boards of education in conducting action research for identifying effective school evaluation methods and professional development for evaluators. In 2007, all the elementary and middle schools implemented self-evaluation and external evaluation, and the Ministry organized a meeting and produced a report to share successful cases of evaluation practices across the country. The purpose of the System is to promote a culture of evaluation and assessment through national support, rather than using the evaluation results for rewards or sanctions.

A comparison of major reforms and policy in the United States, Australia, and Japan shows that all of these countries are moving toward greater standardization and accountability by establishing a standardized national assessment of students and a school evaluation system. However, a major difference emerges when we look at the purpose and implementation of the reforms, especially around accountability, in each country. In the United States, schools and districts are held accountable for student achievement results by public announcement of schools "needing improvement," funding reduction, and a threat of school restructuring. In Australia and Japan, accountability is shared among multiple educational agencies. Assessment results are reported only at the state or prefecture level, and the national government is taking leadership in addressing the key process to improve student learning—supporting schools in engaging in school improvement projects in Australia, and promoting the sharing of successful evaluation methods and supporting the culture of school evaluation for improvement in Japan. Thus, a standardized assessment system is a tool for understanding the nature of student learning and providing support to schools in improving student learning in Australia and Japan. In the United States, standardized assessment is a tool for holding schools and districts accountable, and rewards and sanctions are the mechanisms used for improving student learning.

These reforms have a major impact on teachers' daily working lives. These reforms also influence how teacher policy is developed and implemented for the purpose of improving student learning. We will now turn to the examination and comparison of teacher policy in these three countries.

TEACHER POLICY IN THE UNITED STATES, AUSTRALIA, AND JAPAN

In these policy contexts of increasing standardization and accountability, improving teacher quality is seen as the major vehicle for improving student achievement in all three countries. Such national attention on teachers is manifested in the establishment of federal or national policies or programs: (1) Title II of NCLB in the United States, (2) the Australian Government Quality Teacher Programme, and (3) the Teacher Certification Renewal System in Japan. These are the most influential national policy, program, or system in each country. We will review each of them in detail, but we also will introduce other, less influential national policies or initiatives for teachers.

Title II of No Child Left Behind

Title II of NCLB required that all teachers of core academic subjects be highly qualified by the 2005–06 school year. State departments of education are responsible for developing policies on teacher quality following the NCLB guidelines and for reporting the percentage of highly qualified teachers in each school. In addition, districts are required to report to parents the qualifications of their children's teachers. While these guidelines have been enacted, the criteria for highly qualified teachers were not assessed carefully for their impact on improving the teaching workforce.

Under NCLB, "highly qualified" is defined as fully certified, possessing a bachelor's degree, and demonstrating competence in subject knowledge and teaching. Possession of full certification and a bachelor's degree is fairly straightforward, and all states developed a policy requiring teachers to have these qualifications (Birman et al., 2007). States are given multiple options to choose from to meet the NCLB requirement for content knowledge. States can require teachers to pass national or state assessments in the subject areas they teach, possess a major or minor or a graduate degree in the subject area, complete coursework equivalent to a subject major, or earn an advanced certification or credentials in the subject.

These options have resulted in a significant variation across states in the criteria used to measure teacher competence in content knowledge. All states except two require passing a national or state content knowledge assessment, yet the passing score varies across states. For example, in the Praxis II Assessment in mathematics content knowledge, the passing score ranges from 116 in Arizona to 147 in Virginia (Birman et al., 2007). In addition, for existing teachers, the criteria adopted by the states for meeting the "highly qualified" requirements vary significantly, ranging from simply obtaining a full certification to a performance evaluation using portfolio and observation of instruction by evaluators (Birman et al., 2007).

Under the accountability system of NCLB, states that have failed to meet the highly qualified requirements lose federal funds. The variation in those requirements across states is a natural outcome of states' attempts to avoid financial sanctions by adjusting and often lowering state standards (see also Smith et al., 2005). In addition, lowering the state standards for highly qualified teachers is sometimes the only way to staff inner-city, high-poverty schools, especially in mathematics, science, and special education.

To meet the high demands for teachers in these hard-to-staff schools, many states consider as full certification "provisional," "temporary," or "emergency" certificates given to teacher candidates who have just started teacher training in alternative teacher certification programs.

Since 2005, the U.S. Department of Education has provided Improving Teacher Quality state grants to state departments of education for the purpose of increasing academic achievement by improving teacher and principal quality (U.S. Department of Education, 2008a). Approximately US$2.9 billion has been provided each year, and the funding increased to US$4.4 billion in 2008 for state-determined mechanisms to improve teacher quality, including teacher preparation, recruitment and hiring, induction, professional development, and retention. While this flexibility in the use of funding allows room for innovative state initiatives, a lack of national leadership in promoting a systemic approach to improving teacher quality is likely to result in major variation among states and a lack of coherence within states.

The Australian Government Quality Teacher Programme

The Australian Government Quality Teacher Programme (AGQTP) was established in 1999 for the purpose of improving teacher quality through professional development and improvement of teacher status. The three main objectives of the AGQTP are to (1) equip teachers with the skills and knowledge needed for teaching in the 21st century, (2) provide national leadership in high-priority areas of teacher professional learning need, and (3) improve the professional standing of teachers and school leaders (Australian Government, 2008). The program received funding of A$159 million for the period 1999 to 2004. After favorable evaluation findings for the first phase of the program, a further A$139 million has been allocated for the second phase (2005 to 2009).

The AGQTP has three elements: (1) national projects, (2) state and territory projects, and (3) Teaching Australia. National projects include providing national awards for quality schooling, offering professional development opportunities for teacher leaders and principals, collecting national data on teacher professional learning and supporting teacher quality research, and organizing a national forum for sharing innovative and effective professional learning programs developed by teachers and schools. A national survey revealed that 61% of schools reported that their teachers had participated in a national project on professional development as of 2004 (DEST, 2005). The Australian Government also provides funding to all states and territories, based on the number of teachers, to develop professional development projects that are aligned with state priorities for teacher professional learning and AGQTP priority areas determined by the Australian Government. Since 1999, more than 240,000 teachers have participated in professional learning activities offered through national and state/territory projects (Australian Government, 2008).

Teaching Australia–Australian Institute for Teaching and School Leadership was established in 2003 and subsequently launched in 2005. This is an independent national body for the teaching profession, with the objective of raising the status, quality, and professionalism of teachers and school leaders. Teaching Australia currently is developing a voluntary system for country-wide accreditation of preservice teacher education programs and national professional standards for advanced teaching and school leadership (Teaching Australia, 2007, 2008). It has conducted research on quality teaching and school leadership and disseminated the findings, and organized the Australia Government National Awards for Quality Schooling.

These programs emerged as a remedy for decentralized and fragmented professional development programs and activities across the country. They represent stronger national and state leadership in organizing teachers' learning opportunities and improving teacher status. At the same time, they have structural flexibility so as to allow education authorities to implement professional learning projects that respond to local contexts and identified teacher needs.

An evaluation of the first phase of AGQTP (1999 to 2004) revealed that 75% of participants in AGQTP activities agreed that the activities would lead to a long-term change in teaching practice, and 88% of participants reported that the activities "always" or "sometimes" were targeted to teacher needs (DEST, 2005). However, little evidence was provided for improvement of the status of teaching as a profession as a result of AGQTP activities (DEST, 2005).

Standardization strongly characterizes teacher policy in Australia. The importance of national consistency and leadership is emphasized in every teacher policy document we reviewed. The National Framework for Professional Standards for Teaching was developed in 2003 by the Teacher Quality and Educational Leadership Taskforce in the Ministerial Council on Education, Employment, Training and Youth Affairs (MCEETYA, 2003). The AGQTP, ongoing development of the National Professional Standards for Advanced Teaching and for Principals, and a national accreditation system were initiated after the 1999 Adelaide Declaration on National Goals for Schooling in the 21st Century, which emphasized the importance of enhancing the status and quality of the teaching profession and the development of assessment, accreditation, and credentialing that promote teacher quality (MCEETYA, 1999).

Despite the strong national leadership to seek consistency across the country, these programs were always initiated with a review of both national and international research literature, and consultation and discussion processes with key stakeholders were a major part of policy development. For example, the development of the National Framework for Professional Standards for Teaching was based on the Development Process and Consultative Mechanisms established by the Teacher Quality and Educational Leadership Taskforce (MCEETYA, 2003). The Taskforce consists of representatives from each state or territory, the Australian Government, the National Catholic Education Commission, and the Independent Schools Council of Australia, and it first conducted a thorough review of national and international research and professional standards developed by states/territories, professional associations, and registration bodies to develop a consultation paper on the standards. A national conference was convened in 2002 to engage in discussions on the revisions and improvement of the draft standards, with 79 representatives from states and territories, teacher professional associations, principal associations, and teacher education institutions, as well as researchers and teachers. Major revisions were made based on the recommendations, and the revised standards were distributed nationally for extensive consultation. Written comments and suggestions were integrated to finalize the National Framework for Professional Standards for Teaching.

This type of development and consultation process was used to develop all major national initiatives, and these processes ensured consensus building and support from all key stakeholders. The strong focus, in all national programs, backed by research literature, on supporting professional learning of teachers and improving their professional status also helped gather support from teachers. While the full effects of these national teacher programs are yet to be seen, Australia has successfully mobilized national, state/territory, and local stakeholders to be on board toward higher standards and professionalization of teaching.

Japan's Teacher Certification Renewal System

During the past decade in Japan, teacher quality has gathered both media and policy attention as key to the improvement of student achievement and school attendance and the reduction of school bullying. The need for strengthening teacher education and teacher quality had been discussed by policymakers and researchers since 1990s, and led to the establishment of the Teacher Certification Renewal System in 2007. This system, to be implemented in 2009, abolishes the current permanent certification and requires all new teacher candidates graduating in 2009 and later to renew their certificates every 10 years. Teachers are required to participate in 30 hours of professional development activities, determined by the Ministry of Education, during the 2 years prior to expiration of the certificate, or lose the certificate.

The Ministry stated, "The purpose of the Teacher Certification Renewal System is for teachers to have confidence and pride in teaching and to gain respect and trust of general public through periodically obtaining most recent skills and knowledge and maintaining needed quality and competence" (MEXT, 2008b, p. 10). The focus of this system is to ensure that all teachers are engaged in continuous professional learning by participating in high-quality professional development programs determined by the Ministry and offered by higher education institutions.

Japanese teachers have long devoted tremendous amounts of time to professional development via both formal and informal means. The Education Civil Servant Law requires that first-year teachers and 10th-year teachers spend a minimum of 300 hours for professional development within one year and 200 of those hours need to be spent for out-of-school professional development offered by the Professional Development Centers (MEXT, 2007a). In addition, Lesson Study is widely practiced by Japanese teachers as a teacher-initiated informal learning process. Lesson Study is a process of instructional improvement in which teachers jointly plan, observe, and discuss lessons (Lewis, 2002b), and teachers conduct Lesson Study at least once a month. Lesson Study offers learning opportunities for teachers by focusing on students' thinking processes and allowing them to experiment with instructional approaches and methods in a classroom setting.

The Teacher Certification Renewal System was established as a response to pressure from the public to improve teacher quality, as well as the global trend toward teacher accountability. Ministry officials were aware that teachers were already spending significant amounts of time on professional development, but they responded to public pressure by requiring an additional 30 hours tied to certification renewal as a form of teacher accountability. In reality, adding 30 hours on top of the 300 hours required of 10th-year teachers is not expected to have a major impact. It simply functions as a slight increase in learning opportunities for teachers.

The Ministry also established, in 2006, the Teacher Professional Graduate School System for teachers to seek advanced certification and degrees through practice-based training. The objective was to improve the professional status of teachers and the public trust and respect for teachers (MEXT, 2008b). In 2008, 19 Teacher Professional Graduate Schools were established in 15 national universities and 4 private universities across the country, serving 706 practicing teachers. The missions of these graduate schools are: (1) to train teachers with strong teaching skills and (2) to develop leaders among practicing teachers. At least 40% of the instructors at the Teacher Professional Graduate Schools are required to be practicing teachers who are in leadership positions. The graduate schools also must develop partnerships with local schools for the purpose of promoting the integration of theory and practice. This system was established as an addition to current opportunities to pursue advanced certification and degrees through numerous graduate schools of education across the country. Therefore, the establishment of these Teacher Professional Graduate Schools is unlikely to make a major change to teachers' learning or training opportunities.

Both the Teacher Certification Renewal System and Teacher Professional Graduate School System have the same purpose: to improve teacher quality through more training and continuous professional learning activities. The centralized nature of these reforms means that there was little involvement of key stakeholders, including teacher education institutions, prefecture and local boards of education, school administrators, and teachers, in the development of these reforms. If they become involved, it is clear that these reforms will not have a major impact on the preexisting strong professional learning culture and practices among Japanese teachers, and that instead the focus will shift to the improvement of teachers' working conditions. A major barrier to improving teacher quality lies in teachers' work schedule. A national survey of teachers showed that middle school teachers spend an average of 11.3 hours on scheduled duties and overtime work each day (MEXT, 2007b). Many teachers we interviewed said that they are overworked, which leaves less and less time for professional learning. If the Ministry aims to truly improve teacher quality, it needs to implement a reform to dramatically improve teacher workload rather than simply increasing the required professional development hours.

Comparison of Teacher Policy in Three Countries

A major difference between the Title II requirements of the NCLB and both the AGQTP and Japanese Teacher Certification Renewal System is a different assumption about the process to improve teacher quality. NCLB focuses on the entry-level qualification, while the AGQTP and Teacher Certification Renewal System focus on continuous professional development and improving teacher status. Although under NCLB federal funds are provided to state departments of education to improve teacher quality, no structural reform of the fragmented nature of professional development activities or the huge inequality in school resources across school districts was implemented. There is no mention of improving teacher status or working conditions in NCLB other than the promotion of performance-based compensation systems, but no consideration is given to the major differences in working conditions between high-SES and low-SES schools reported by previous studies (Kozol, 1992, 2005). The gap in student access to qualified teachers between high-SES and low-SES schools in the United States is the fourth largest among 39 countries (Akiba et al., 2007).

Previous studies have shown that in the United States successful state or district reforms to systematically improve teacher quality and student learning have been limited to a small number of states and districts (Darling-Hammond & Sykes, 2003), and that most state reforms lack coherence and systemic approaches (Fuhrman, 1993; Fuhrman et al., 2007). These studies pointed out the importance of developing a coherent policy based on student and teacher standards for improving teacher quality and student learning and the importance of the federal role in supporting the conditions for promoting a coherent policy. NCLB set the requirements for states to follow—to allow only "highly qualified" candidates to enter teaching. However, it did not address the root problems of teacher quality, which, among others, are unbalanced teacher labor markets that create a major teacher shortage in inner-city, high-poverty schools; the fragmented nature of teacher learning opportunities; and unattractive working conditions compared with other professions (National Commission on Teaching and America's Future, 1996). As a result, NCLB created major variation in the operational definition of "highly qualified" teachers across the states. It does little to actually improve the quality of teachers as it does not address the root problems underlying teacher quality in the United States.

Both Australia's and Japan's teacher reforms have focused on professional development as the key process for improving teacher quality. Thus, the purpose of these reforms is to provide high-quality learning opportunities to all teachers based on the visions of high-quality teachers. In Australia, professional development activities are offered by multiple agencies, including teacher education institutions, professional associations, state/territory departments of education, teacher unions, and schools. The learning opportunities have been largely fragmented, with little coherence or alignment among activities. The AGQTP is the national initiative to structure professional development activities based on national and state priorities and standards. To build consensus and support for the common goal of improving teacher quality and student learning, all key stakeholders were involved in the development and implementation processes. In Japan, teacher learning opportunities are well structured, and a national framework that aligns both formal and informal professional development activities is shared among all key stakeholders (see Chapter 5). Yet, the new teacher reforms were developed and implemented without involving key stakeholders, and as a result the impact of these reforms is likely to be minimal. Despite this limitation, the Japanese Government fully supports the professional learning of teachers as the main vehicle for improving the quality of the teaching profession.

Another major process for improving teacher quality—improvement of teachers' working conditions—has not been addressed thoroughly in any of the three countries. While improving the status of the teaching profession is an important goal of teacher reforms and policy in both Australia and Japan, improvement of working conditions was not part of the reforms or policy implementation in either country. In Australia, the Australian Education Union and its state/territory branches play a major role in improving working conditions, including teacher salary, allowance, and paid leave. In Japan, national legislation has maintained teachers' salaries higher than those of other civil servants, but teachers' workload needs major improvement. These working conditions and related policy and practices are investigated in Chapter 4.

Coherence in teacher policy is critical for systematically reforming the complex, multidimensional processes for improving teacher quality. All the processes that impact teacher quality—recruitment of high-quality candidates into teaching, teacher education and training, hiring and distribution, teacher working conditions, and teacher induction and professional development—need to be aligned to achieve the common goal agreed upon and supported by all key stakeholders. This process starts with establishing a vision of high-quality teachers, which is culturally bound as teacher roles differ across various historical, cultural, and societal contexts. How are the characteristics of high-quality teachers alike or different across the United States, Australia, and Japan?

TEACHERS' ROLE: A VISION OF HIGH-QUALITY TEACHERS

What characterizes high-quality teachers is highly contested. Within each of the three nations, there is wide variation in terms of what people think are the characteristics of good teachers. Therefore, it is a mistake to think that there is one vision of high-quality teachers that is shared by everyone in each country that policymakers can readily utilize. Rather, part of the development of any coherent policy for the teaching force must be the active development of a set of broadly agreed-upon characteristics of high-quality teachers. We focused on dominant characteristics developed by teacher professional associations and described in teacher professional standards in the United States and Australia. In Japan, we relied on statements on teacher quality and competence in a major document developed by the Ministry of Education. Table 2.2 presents the core statements on the characteristics of high-quality teachers in teacher professional standards in the United States and Australia and in a government document in Japan. The NBPTS in the United States is an independent, nonprofit, nongovernmental organization funded by Carnegie Corporation of New York and developed and operated by teachers. It developed rigorous professional teaching standards called "What Teachers Should Know and Be Able to Do" (NBPTS, 1994), and it offers a voluntary advanced certificate to experienced teachers. Across the country, more than 55,000 teachers are National Board Certified Teachers, and 25% of school districts offer financial rewards or incentives for experienced teachers to become certified through the NBPTS (n.d.). The NBPTS has been modeled in national standards for beginning teachers developed by the INTASC (1992) and in many state standards for professional teaching.

The National Professional Standards for Advanced Teaching and for Principals currently are being developed by Teaching Australia. They consist of the charter for the Australian teaching profession and "advanced teaching capabilities" and "principal capabilities" under the charter (Teaching Australia, 2008). The purposes are to increase public recognition of the quality of the profession, develop a common language for discussing professional practice, and use the standards to identify accomplished professional performance. Advanced teaching capabilities were developed by a group of teachers in national professional associations in November 2007, and feedback currently is being sought from key stakeholders across the nation. "Descriptors of accomplishments" that specify indicators of capabilities also are being developed.

In Japan, a vision of high-quality teachers described in "Quality and Competence Needed for Teachers," developed by the Ministry of Education, is widely distributed and shared among administrators and teachers (MEXT, 2008b). The lack of teacher professional standards in Japan is probably because teachers share common ideas of high-quality teachers growing out of the country's collaborative professional learning culture (Shimahara, 2002; Shimahara & Sakai, 1995) and there is no need to seek consensus through the development of professional standards. Until the teacher reforms of the past few years, the Ministry of Education did not speak to the issue of teacher quality. The characteristics described in this government document are likely to reflect the shared vision of good teachers in the teaching profession.

Table 2.2. National statements on "high-quality teachers" in the United States, Australia, and Japan.

United States: National Board for Professional Teaching Standards (1994)	Australia: National Professional Standards for Advanced Teaching and for Principals (2008)	Japan: Quality and Competence Needed for Teachers (2008)
1. Teachers are committed to students and their learning.	1. Contemporary and authoritative professional knowledge and understanding of:	1. Strong passion for teaching: Commitment and pride in teaching and love and responsibility for students
2. Teachers know the subjects they teach and how to teach those subjects to students.	1.1. Students and the factors that influence learning and development	2. Competence as an education expert: Understanding of students, skills for student guidance, "shudan shido", and classroom community development
3. Teachers are responsible for managing and monitoring student learning.	1.2. Effective pedagogies, assessment and reporting	3. Holistic humanity: Rich humanity and social skills, general knowledge, communication skills including courtesy and social manners
4. Teachers think systematically about their practice and learn from experience.	1.3. Areas of specialization and expertise	
5. Teachers are members of learning communities.	1.4. A wide range of resources, including emerging technologies, and their use in teaching and learning	
	2. Exemplary professional practice, applying contemporary and authoritative professional knowledge to:	
	2.1. Build effective relationships and manage complex interactions	
	2.2. Create and maintain intellectually challenging learning environments	
	2.3. Design, implement and evaluate rigorous and inclusive learning programs	
	2.4. Use purposeful assessment and feedback to inform teaching and learning	
	2.5. Communicate effectively with different audiences using a repertoire of strategies	
	3. Inspiring and influential professional leadership to:	
	3.1. Initiate, evaluate and respond to change	
	3.2. Engage in critical reflection to improve their own and their colleagues' practice	
	3.3. Work collegially, valuing the contribution of others, fostering strategic partnerships and stimulating professional discussion	
	3.4. Encourage an environment of confidence and resilience	
	3.5. Take responsibility for the development and renewal of the profession	

A comparison of the core statements on high-quality teachers in Table 2.2 shows both similarities and differences among the United States, Australia, and Japan. The major similarity is that the statements in all three countries speak to teachers' knowledge, skills/practice, and disposition. Teachers' knowledge of students, skills in teaching or educating them and creating effective learning environments, and commitment to students and teaching are addressed in the statements in all three countries.

We also can see several differences. First, in the U.S. and Australian standards, the importance of "reflection" and "collaboration" is addressed, but these concepts are absent in the Japanese document. The NBPTS's fourth statement, "Teachers think systematically about their practice and learn from experience," and Australian Standard 3.2, "engage in critical reflection to improve their own and their colleagues' practice," address the importance of reflection. The importance of collaboration is addressed by NBPTS's fifth statement, "Teachers are members of learning communities," and Australian Standard 3.3, "work collegially, valuing the contribution of others, fostering strategic partnerships and stimulating professional discussion." These dispositions of teachers are considered as ideals in the United States and Australia and as traits that all high-quality teachers should seek to possess. These concepts do not appear in the Japanese statements, probably because they are norms among Japanese teachers (LeTendre, 2000; Shimahara & Sakai, 1995; Stigler & Hiebert, 1999).

Second, U.S. and Australian statements of high-quality teachers focus on "learning," while Japanese statements focus on "education." The word *learning* or *learn* appears four times in the U.S. statements and five times in the Australian standards. This word, which is translated as *manabi* or *gakushu* in Japanese, does not appear in the Japanese statements. The teachers' role in student learning is only a part of their overall educational role, and the focus on broader "education" is expressed in the second quality for teachers, "competence as an education expert." The competence is specified further as skills for student guidance, characterized by student counseling for both academic and social issues, *shudan shido* (teaching of collective values and behaviors), and classroom community development. None of these roles are focused on classroom instruction, and instead they focus on whole child education that promotes social, psychological, physical, and academic development. Teachers' multiple roles in whole child education in Japan have been well documented in previous comparative studies (LeTendre, 2000; Lewis, 1995; Shimahara & Sakai, 1995).

Third, the Australian and Japanese statements have unique elements that were not found in the U.S. statements. The Australian Professional Standards address the importance of encouraging "an environment of confidence and resilience" (among teachers) as well as taking "responsi-bility for the development and renewal of the profession" (Standards 3.4 and 3.5). As these statements were developed by Australian teachers, these elements may reflect their commitment to improving the status of the teaching profession through professional leadership and responsibil-ity. The focus on "holistic humanity" as a quality of teachers in the Japa-nese statement is also unique. The concepts of compassion, sympathy, and thoughtfulness toward others are a major part of humanity, and these are the dispositions ideally possessed by Japanese teachers as well as im-portant characteristics teachers instill in students (Tobin, Wu, & Davidson, 1989).

In summary, visions of high-quality teachers in the United States, Australia, and Japan have both a common feature as well as differences. All statements share the importance of teacher knowledge, skills, and commitment to teaching and students. However, the specific focus within these general characteristics differs due to the cultural idea of teachers' roles as well as the traits currently lacking among teachers. The cultural role of Japanese teachers—to engage in whole-person education—is con-trasted with the major role in classroom instruction among U.S. and Aus-tralian teachers. The importance of collaboration and reflection are shared in all three countries, but these concepts do not appear in the Japanese statements as they are norms of the teaching profession. These visions of high-quality teachers influence the discourse and debate on the roles of teachers and the direction and nature of educational policy and systems for improving teacher quality. These visions of high-quality teachers also serve as the goals of teacher policy, and the extent to which they are shared among key stakeholders determines the coherence of teacher policy and the success of teacher policy implementation.

SUMMARY

Comparisons of national contexts, major educational reforms, and teacher policy in the United States, Australia, and Japan show that no country is free from the global forces that shape reforms and policy. There are major differences in the teacher and student population sizes, language diver-sity, and education governance structure and public school funding sources, yet all three countries' educational reforms are characterized by the global trends toward standardization and accountability. All three coun-tries have established a national student assessment system, and national standards have been developed. The national or federal government's in-volvement in education has increased over the years, and the government increasingly has invested in the improvement of the teaching workforce as the driving force for economic success in all three countries.

Yet, we also see a major difference in the approaches of each country toward improving the quality of the teaching workforce. The U.S. teacher policy is uniquely different from that of Australia and Japan in its focus on "requirements" rather than "support." Accountability is delegated to districts and schools without major federal or state support to address the root problems of unequal distribution of qualified teachers, fragmented professional learning opportunities, and unattractive working conditions. In Australia and Japan accountability is shared, with assessment results used for identifying the locus and nature of support rather than for rewards and sanctions.

A comparison of national statements on "high-quality teachers" also showed both a similarity in structure and differences in content. The similarity in structure, focusing on teacher knowledge, skills, and disposition, was likely a result of international research conducted during the development process of these national standards—a process through which global forces influenced the direction of each country's educational reforms. Yet, the development of the content of what "good teachers" look like was deeply influenced by the cultural roles of teachers as well as the existing system, organization, and norms surrounding teachers.

In Chapters 3 through 5, we will examine carefully the major processes of improving teacher quality: teacher recruitment, hiring, and distribution (Chapter 3), working conditions (Chapter 4), and professional learning opportunities (Chapter 5). Each chapter starts with the examination of the current state of teacher quality, working conditions, and learning opportunities. Then, policy and processes that are in place in each country to maintain or improve teacher quality are carefully examined and compared. The interaction between global forces and local culture and priorities is revealed in the development of uniquely different policy and processes for improving teacher quality among the United States, Australia, and Japan.

CHAPTER 3

Teacher Quality and Workforce Planning and Management

DURING THE PAST 50 years the United States has seen a host of educational reforms aimed at improving the quality of schools, access to education, and the overall quality of instruction that students receive. As discussed in Chapters 1 and 2, however, the focus of these reforms was rarely the teachers themselves. Scholars like Hirsch (1987) advocated an exclusive focus on the curriculum, the establishment of "standards," and the promotion of rigorous testing programs that some have argued alienate teachers from the curriculum itself. Cross-national work by the International Association for the Evaluation of Educational Achievement (IEA) also focused heavily on the curriculum (Schmidt et al., 2001), providing subject analysis to the topic-level curriculum content in an attempt to further understand how the curriculum affects student learning.

Research in the past 15 years increasingly has shifted from a focus on the ideal curriculum, to a focus on the "enacted" curriculum, or OTL (Dougherty, 1996; Wang, 1998). This shift has reawakened an interest in classroom processes, instructional practice, and teacher quality. The change in emphasis from the ideal to the implemented curriculum has brought teachers to the forefront of debates about international achievement and has made teacher "quality" a topic of intense policy interest. Both the federal government and independent academic groups (e.g., the National Academies) see teacher quality as the crucial driving force for improving student achievement and thus promoting the nation's economic competitiveness in a global society. In a 2006 annual report on teacher quality, Secretary of Education Margaret Spellings stated:

> In order to strengthen our nation's competitiveness in the global marketplace, as well as our security at home, we must be certain that teacher proficiency in mathematics, science, technology, and foreign languages is sufficient to enable America's students to achieve at grade level and above in these subjects. (U.S. Department of Education, 2006, p. iii)

The importance of teacher quality also is noted by the National Academies (2007) in Web information on its Study of Teacher Preparation Programs: "Teacher quality is widely recognized by policymakers, practitioners, and researchers alike to be the most powerful school-related influence on a child's academic performance."

DOES TEACHER QUALIFICATION LEAD TO IMPROVED STUDENT ACHIEVEMENT?

In the United States, many empirical studies have been conducted to identify characteristics of teacher quality that are associated with higher student achievement. Several scholars have attempted to synthesize these studies and have identified teacher certification, subject-matter knowledge, pedagogical knowledge, and teaching experience as significantly associated with higher achievement or greater achievement gains among students (Darling-Hammond & Youngs, 2002; Rice, 2003; Wayne & Youngs, 2003; Wilson, Floden, & Ferrini-Mundy, 2001, 2002). However, apart from the identification of these rather broad areas, little consensus has formed on just what teacher quality is and what policies would promote it.

Just attempting to define teacher quality can raise serious arguments among educators and scholars, and attempts to implement teacher quality regulations under NCLB have already been challenged in the courts (Peckham, 2007). For some, any attempt to standardize and measure the training of teachers and its impact on student learning (as measured in test scores) smacks of a heavy-handed governmental imposition that denies the highly nuanced relationships between "quality" teachers and their students. These criticisms, while often carried to extremes, provide an important reminder that improvements in student test scores measure only a fraction of the work that teachers are expected to do. While all teachers can reasonably be expected to have subject-specialty mastery and high instructional quality as part of their core professional expectations, teachers at different levels play many different roles and employ a wide range of instructional practices that make comparison a challenge.

Policymakers at the state and national levels do not have the luxury of engaging in such fine comparisons. Since the Johnson administration, national educational policy typically has focused on basic measures of educational attainment and access (Stein, 2004). Even before NCLB, policymakers tended to rely heavily on the standardized assessments of student outcomes reported by the National Assessment of Educational Progress (NAEP), and it is only within the past few years that states (such as South

Carolina and Kansas) have begun collecting detailed data on broader issues such as teacher working conditions.

Measuring teacher quality across various national contexts poses complicated methodological and policy challenges to understanding teacher quality. Each country defines "high-quality teacher" differently, as shown in Chapter 2. Many comparative studies also have shown that the cultural roles and identities of teachers vary across countries (Anderson-Levitt, 2005; LeTendre, 1994, 1995; Shimahara & Sakai, 1995; Welmond, 2002). National patterns of school organization and political priorities also affect teachers' work roles and approaches to teaching (LeTendre et al., 2001a; Osborn et al., 2003).

However, the past century has witnessed considerable homogenization of national curricula within core subject areas (Benavot & Braslavsky, 2006; Benavot, Cha, Kamens, Meyer, & Wong, 1991). Work by "neo-institutionalist" scholars (Meyer, Ramirez, & Soysal, 1992; Ramirez & Boli, 1987) shows a long-term, transnational trend toward isomorphism in core curriculum and basic instructional practices. Although scholars continue to debate the extent to which teaching is affected by national cultures or a global cultural dynamic (see Anderson-Levitt, 2005; Givvin, Hiebert, Jacobs, Hollingsworth, & Gallimore, 2005; LeTendre et al., 2001a), it is clear that for highly structured subjects such as mathematics, teachers around the world readily can recognize (and critique) core curricular concepts and instructional strategies across a wide range of nations (Stigler & Hiebert, 1999). There also has been a strong institutionalization of developmental norms globally, so that teachers at any given level (preschool, elementary school, middle school) are likely to share many beliefs about basic learning needs (Olmsted & Weikert, 1989). If we are careful to compare teachers who teach the same subject at the same level, we can better identify how teachers in various nations differ in their education and training, and what impact this has on student achievement. In this book, we have focused on a single level (8th grade) and a single subject area (mathematics).

We have taken the stance that all teachers have student learning as a core concern. But we also hypothesize that their education, their working conditions, and the institutional environment of the school system affect how they perceive student learning and how they attempt to get students to learn. We also recognize that national policymakers will be constrained to focus on a few key measures. Thus we decided to use measurable characteristics of teacher qualifications (from the TIMSS teacher survey data) that have been linked with student achievement in past studies and that share a relatively common meaning across various cultural contexts:

- Full certification
- Mathematics major
- Mathematics education major
- Teaching experience of 3 or more years

In addition to these four separate measures of teacher quality, we developed an overall measure of teacher quality:

- Percentage of students taught by mathematics teachers who are fully certified, who majored in mathematics or mathematics education, and who have 3 or more years of teaching experience

In our previous work, we found that students in countries with higher teacher quality achieved higher scores than students in countries with lower teacher quality when the GDP per capita and educational expenditure as a percentage of GDP were held constant (Akiba et al., 2007). Evidence from U.S. studies as well as this cross-national study showed that teacher quality is a critical factor in improving student achievement. Previous studies, however, have not investigated how policy contexts surrounding teacher quality explain differences in the level of teacher quality and distribution of qualified teachers. To begin to provide a national baseline for comparison, in this chapter we will compare the level of teacher qualification in the United States, Australia, and Japan based on the measures listed above. We also will show how teacher quality differs between wealthy and high-poverty schools. Then, we will compare and discuss teacher recruitment policy and practice to attract qualified candidates into teaching, and hiring and distribution policy to equalize student access to qualified teachers in the United States, Australia, and Japan. We will close the chapter with policy recommendations for improving the quality of the U.S. teacher workforce.

COMPARING TEACHER QUALITY IN
THE UNITED STATES AND ABROAD

Full Certification

Teacher certification demonstrates that a teacher candidate has completed the required teacher education credit hours or has demonstrated a level of professional skill in a related field commensurate with certification (see Humphrey, Wechsler, & Hough, 2008, for an analysis of the effectiveness of alternative certification programs). In the United States, Australia, and

Japan, the vast majority of teachers obtain certification by completing traditional teacher education programs. In the United States, independent national accreditation organizations (i.e., the National Council for Accreditation and Teacher Education and Teacher Education Accreditation Council) and state departments of education are responsible for reviewing and approving teacher education curricula. In Australia, state and territory teacher registration authorities (e.g., New South Wales Institute of Teachers, Victorian Institute of Teaching) conduct accreditation of teacher education programs, and a national accreditation process currently is being developed (Teaching Australia, 2007). In Japan, the Council for Educational Personnel Training, an organization under the Ministry of Education, is responsible for teacher education curriculum. Despite the difference in the locus of accreditation agencies, the content of the teacher education curriculum is strikingly similar.

In all three countries, the curriculum consists of four elements: (1) general education, (2) subject content, (3) pedagogy and methods, and (4) student teaching. In the United States, successful passage of the state teacher licensing examination is required for certification in addition to completion of required coursework, and most states use the Praxis II, which assesses content knowledge in the Praxis Series: Professional Assessments for Beginning Teachers. Each year America's colleges and universities graduate about 200,000 teachers (Rotherham & Mead, 2004) who are eligible for state certification and, through reciprocal state agreements, often are able to transfer their certification to neighboring states. In Australia and Japan, completion of required coursework will grant certification.

Based on these criteria, what percentage of practicing teachers possess full certification? One may wonder how teachers can be allowed to teach without a teaching certification. Despite the commonsense understanding that all teachers should be fully certified, the reality of teacher shortages in the United States and so many other countries forces educational authorities to allow individuals without full certification to teach in school (Peckham, 2007). Our work on the comparison of 39 countries showed that on average, about 9% of eighth-grade mathematics teachers internationally are teaching without a teaching certification (Akiba et al., 2007). What does the percentage look like in the United States, Australia, and Japan?

Figure 3.1 shows the percentage of eighth-grade mathematics teachers who are teaching mathematics with a full teaching certification in the United States, Australia, and Japan based on the teacher survey report in the 2003 TIMSS data set. The average of eight other countries with higher national achievement than the United States also is reported as a comparison (four other higher achieving countries did not report this information). The TIMSS data did not specify whether the certification was for mathematics or not. Therefore these percentages include mathematics teachers with a full certification in another subject area. Despite this data limitation, the percentages show the level of implementation of the certification requirement for teaching. In the United States, 95.1% of mathematics teachers possess a full certification, slightly lower than the 95.8% in Australia. In Japan, 99.4% hold a full certification, which shows the close-to-universal implementation of the certification requirement for entry into teaching. The percentage of the United States and Australia is similar to that of the average of eight other high-achieving countries.

As a basic measure of policy impact, the U.S. teaching force appears about average in terms of certification. The vast majority of U.S. teachers involved with 8th-grade math have certification, indicating a near-universal adherence to policy recommendations. This does not mean that the certifications of all teachers are equal, or that simply being certified means that effective instruction is being given in classrooms. But it does mean that the basic mechanisms of educating and supplying teachers are

Figure 3.1. Percentage of eighth-grade mathematics teachers with full certification.

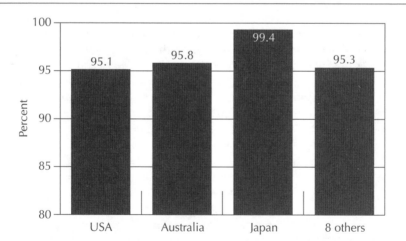

Notes: "8 others" indicates average percentage of Estonia, Hong Kong, Malaysia, the Russian Federation, Singapore, the Slovak Republic, South Korea, and Taiwan. No data were provided by Belgium (Flemish), Hungary, Latvia, and the Netherlands. All figures in this chapter from TIMSS database.

not dramatically lower in the United States than in higher performing countries.

Subject Major

Possessing a subject major demonstrates that a teacher candidate completed subject-specific content courses. For mathematics teachers, those who majored in mathematics mastered college-level mathematics and possess in-depth knowledge in mathematics. Those who majored in mathematics education further mastered how to teach mathematics to students as well as general pedagogy-related courses (e.g., educational psychology, child development). Previous studies have demonstrated that students who were taught mathematics by teachers with an undergraduate or graduate mathematics major made greater achievement gains than those who were taught mathematics by teachers with a nonmath major or degree (Goldhaber & Brewer, 1997, 2000; Rowan, Chiang, & Miller, 1997). Thus, subject major is an important indicator of teacher quality that leads to improved student achievement.

Figure 3.2 shows the percentage of eighth-grade mathematics teachers who answered yes to one of the following questions on the 2003 TIMSS survey: "During your postsecondary education, was 'mathematics' your major or main area(s) of study?" and "During your postsecondary education, was 'mathematics education' your major or main area(s) of study?" Of U.S. teachers, 70.3% reported that they majored in mathematics or mathematics education. This percentage is slightly lower than the 73.6% in Australia, and significantly lower than the 87.9% in Japan. The average of 12 other high-achieving countries was 88.9%, which is significantly higher than the percentages of the United States and Australia. This shows that close to 90% of teachers possess a math or math education major in Japan and 12 other high-achieving countries.

When we further broke down the percentages for mathematics major and mathematics education major, we found that in the United States 24.4% majored in mathematics only, 17.2% majored in mathematics education only, and 28.7% majored in both mathematics and mathematics education. The percentages in Australia are 15.8, 11.8, and 46.0, respectively, and the percentages in Japan are 29.2, 6.8, and 51.9, respectively, for mathematics major, mathematics education major, and both majors. We can see that 46.0% of Australian mathematics teachers and 51.9% of Japanese mathematics teachers majored both in mathematics and mathematics education, compared with only 28.7% among U.S. mathematics teachers.

Figure 3.2. Percentage of eighth-grade mathematics teachers with mathematics or mathematics education major.

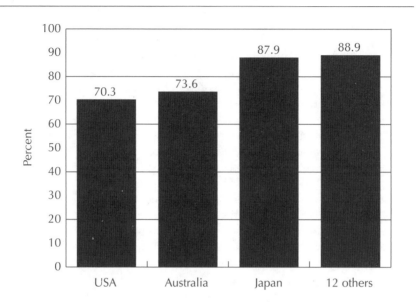

Note: "12 others" indicates average percentage of Belgium (Flemish), Estonia, Hong Kong, Hungary, Latvia, Malaysia, the Netherlands, the Russian Federation, Singapore, the Slovak Republic, South Korea, and Taiwan.

Approximately 30% of U.S. teachers and 26% of Australian teachers are teaching mathematics without a mathematics or mathematics education major. While the majority of these teachers are fully certified based on the data in Figure 3.1, they may not hold a mathematics certification. This is likely a reflection of teacher shortages in these countries. Mathematics is reported to be one of the subject areas with the greatest teacher shortage in both countries (Birman et al., 2007). When U.S. school districts or Australian state departments of education cannot find teachers who hold mathematics certification to teach in middle schools, they have no choice but to assign out-of-field teachers to teach mathematics. Approximately 30% of U.S. teachers and 26% of Australian teachers may be teaching mathematics to fill vacancies in mathematics teacher positions. In contrast, in Japan, there is a general oversupply of teacher candidates, and only 14% of applicants were hired as teachers during 2007 (MEXT, 2008b). An oversupply of teacher candidates also exists in some of the other high-achieving countries, including Taiwan, South Korea, Hong Kong, and Singapore.

Teaching Experience

Another indicator of teacher quality is teaching experience. If teacher learning accumulates with years of teaching practice, experienced teachers should be more effective than novice teachers in improving student achievement. Many empirical studies have, indeed, shown a significant and positive relationship between number of years teaching and student achievement (see reviews by Greenwald, Hedges, & Laine, 1996, and Rice, 2003). However, the relationship is not linear. Teachers' effectiveness in improving student achievement appears to increase in the first 3 years of teaching, but no major improvement in their effectiveness was observed after 3 years of teaching experience (Boyd, Grossman, Lankford, Loeb, & Wyckoff, 2006; Rice, 2003; Rivkin, Hanushek, & Kain, 2005).

We examined the percentage of eighth-grade mathematics teachers who have 3 or more years of teaching experience, as reported by the TIMSS survey (Figure 3.3). Overall, all three nations have very experienced teaching forces. In the United States and Australia, about 90% of teachers have 3 or more years of teaching experience, and these percentages are similar to that of the average of 12 other high-achieving countries. In Japan, the percentage is 96.3%, which is significantly higher than in most other nations. Whether this difference helps to improve Japanese student achievement overall is unclear, and we would caution policymakers from placing too much emphasis on this difference when the vast majority of teachers (i.e., 90%) in many nations have more than 3 years of experience.

We would focus rather on the implications of these numbers for the overall teaching force. The United States has very high turnover, or attrition, in its teacher force during the first few years of teaching, but those teachers who make it through this period appear to stay for a significant amount of time. This suggests the importance of systemic induction and mentoring programs if we are to build long-term professional excellence in the teaching force.

Overall Teacher Quality

When we examine teacher quality, it is also important to look at multiple indicators to measure its complex nature. Therefore, we computed the percentage of eighth-grade mathematics teachers who hold a full certification, who majored in mathematics or mathematics education, and who have 3 or more years of teaching experience. The results are presented in Figure 3.4. In the United States, 63.7% of mathematics teachers are considered qualified teachers based on these criteria. A slightly higher percentage, 68.7, met these criteria in Australia. In Japan, 83.5%

Figure 3.3. Percentage of eighth-grade mathematics teachers with 3 or more years of teaching experience.

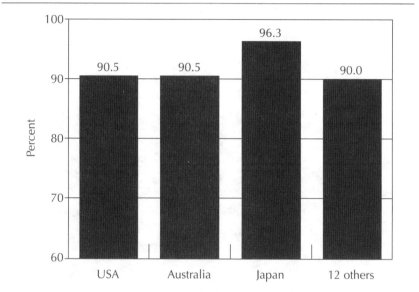

Note: "12 others" indicates average percentage of Belgium (Flemish), Estonia, Hong Kong, Hungary, Latvia, Malaysia, the Netherlands, the Russian Federation, Singapore, the Slovak Republic, South Korea, and Taiwan.

of mathematics teachers are considered qualified teachers, a percentage that is higher than those for the United States, Australia, and the average of 8 other high-achieving countries (76.4%).

In the United States, approximately 36% of mathematics teachers do not hold a full certification, have a math or math education major, or have 3 or more years of teaching experience. As these characteristics of teacher qualification were empirically shown to predict higher student achievement, it is critical to take a systemic approach to improving the overall qualification of the United States teaching force.

THE TEACHER QUALITY GAP BETWEEN
HIGH- AND LOW-POVERTY SCHOOLS

Another important characteristic of the overall teaching workforce that impacts student achievement is the distribution of qualified teachers across schools with various levels of socioeconomic wealth. In a country like the

Figure 3.4. Percentage of eighth-grade mathematics teachers with a full certification, mathematics or mathematics education major, and 3 years of teaching experience.

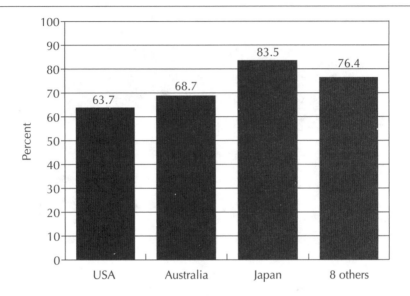

Note: "8 others" indicates average percentage of Estonia, Hong Kong, Malaysia, the Russian Federation, Singapore, the Slovak Republic, South Korea, and Taiwan. No data were provided by Belgium (Flemish), Hungary, Latvia, and the Netherlands.

United States, where there are huge funding differences between wealthy and high-poverty districts, it is often difficult to ensure that students receive equal access to qualified teachers. To examine the level of access to qualified teachers across schools of various socioeconomic status, we computed the percentage of qualified teachers (with a full certification, a math or math education major, and 3 or more years of teaching experience) in the bottom one-third (low-SES) and top one-third (high-SES) of schools, based on the average socioeconomic status of students. The results are presented in Figure 3.5.

The figure shows a striking difference in teacher qualification between low-SES schools and high-SES schools in the United States. While 75.0% of teachers in high-SES schools are considered qualified teachers, only 51.9% of teachers are qualified teachers in low-SES schools. The gap between low-SES and high-SES schools also exists in Australia, but it is only 8.5% (67.7 vs. 59.2), a significantly smaller gap than the 23.1% gap in

Figure 3.5. Percentage of eighth-grade mathematics teachers with a full certification, mathematics or mathematics education major, and 3 or more years of teaching experience in low-SES and high-SES schools.

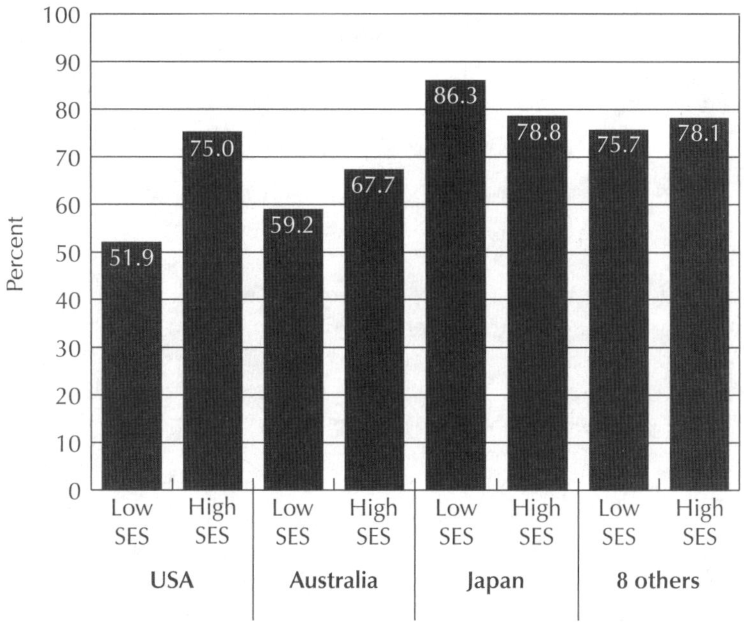

Note: "8 others" indicates average percentage of Estonia, Hong Kong, Malaysia, the Russian Federation, Singapore, the Slovak Republic, South Korea, and Taiwan. No data were provided by Belgium (Flemish), Hungary, Latvia, and the Netherlands.

the United States. In Japan, an opposite pattern was observed: Low-SES schools have a higher percentage (86.3%) of qualified teachers than do high-SES schools (78.8%).

The gap between low-SES and high-SES schools was small for the average of eight other high-achieving countries: only 2.4% (75.7 vs. 78.1). This shows that a majority of high-achieving countries, including Japan, are successful in balancing teacher quality between wealthy and high-poverty schools. Our previous study, which compared the opportunity gap—the difference in percentage of students taught by qualified teachers between low-SES and high-SES schools—showed that the opportunity gap in the United States was the fourth largest among 39 countries around the world (Akiba et al., 2007).

In summary, the level of overall teacher quality in the United States is significantly lower than in Japan and other high-achieving countries, and the gap in teacher quality between low-SES and high-SES schools in the United States is larger than in Australia, Japan, and other high-achieving countries. What explains the high teacher quality in Japan? What do Australia and Japan do to achieve equity in the distribution of qualified teachers? What can U.S. policymakers do to improve the quality of the teaching workforce and distribute qualified teachers equally?

THE IMPORTANCE OF WORKFORCE PLANNING AND MANAGEMENT

The quality of the teaching force is determined by successful workforce planning to attract the most qualified individuals into the teaching profession, and workforce management to retain qualified teachers through providing attractive working conditions and professional learning opportunities (Smylie & Miretzky, 2004). In the countries experiencing a teacher shortage, a systemic approach to recruiting, hiring, distributing, and retaining qualified teachers is critical. Fundamental to the development of such a systemic approach is the availability of workforce data: an understanding of where the shortage exists (school levels and subject areas) compared with the specialization of teacher candidates, data on attrition and mobility of the teaching workforce, and comprehensive information on qualified teacher candidates who are available but not currently employed. This is critical information for developing a systemic approach to address teacher shortage.

The major difference between the United States and Australia or Japan lies in the level of workforce planning and management. In the United States, teacher recruitment, hiring, and retention are practiced by school districts and schools (Liu & Johnson, 2006), whereas in Australia and Japan, these are responsibilities of state departments of education or prefecture boards of education—the education agencies with the same level of authority as the state departments of education in the United States. While school district operation of education is aligned with the principle of decentralized control, this decentralized system creates multiple problems in workforce planning and management.

First, because school districts and schools do not have access to statewide data on teacher labor market trends and characteristics, their hiring process is reactive to the number of applicants each year rather than a proactive process to project long-term trends. This prevents them from taking a systemic approach that targets the areas of teacher shortage based on long-term trends of teacher labor markets. A survey of 486 first- and second-year teachers in California, Florida, Massachusetts, and Michigan (Liu & Johnson, 2006) found that a majority of teachers were hired within the month before the school year started or after the school year started and had limited interactions with school personnel during the hiring process. This indicates that most districts and schools take reactive and non-systematic approaches to hiring teachers.

Second, each district or school is concerned with recruiting qualified teachers only for itself. As school districts and schools differ in their capacity to attract highly qualified teachers, this creates inequality in the distribution of teachers among school districts and schools, especially between wealthy ones and high-poverty ones. While two-thirds of high-minority, high-poverty, and urban districts are challenged by inadequate teacher salaries and competition with other districts, less than half of other districts face the same challenges, according to a national survey of school districts (Birman et al., 2007). This survey clearly shows that high-poverty urban districts and schools are disadvantaged in the competition and their children are most likely to suffer from lack of access to qualified teachers.

Third, due to the difference in hiring processes among districts, teacher candidates need to send in different packets of applications, follow up with each district that has a different selection process, and prepare for different types of interviews. The timing of job offers also varies from district to district. This process can discourage qualified candidates from pursuing teaching if other job options are available to them. Because districts that lack resources are more likely to have a disorganized hiring process and limited human resources, they are at a disadvantage in attracting qualified candidates.

A study of four "hard-to-staff" urban districts reported that 31 to 58% of applicants withdrew their applications and accepted jobs from other, wealthier districts mainly because of the late hiring timelines of July or August (Levin & Quinn, 2003). This study pointed out three policy barriers that cause late hiring: (1) vacancy notification requirements that allow teachers a late notice of their intent to leave, (2) teacher union transfer agreements that require schools to hire transferring teachers before new teachers, and (3) late budget timetables and inadequate forecasting that allow uncertainty about available funded positions to remain until late in the hiring cycle. Levin and Quinn (2003) offered the following solution:

- Revising teacher requirements for early notification
- Expediting the teacher transfer process and enabling schools to consider both external and internal candidates equally

- Promoting earlier and more predictable budgets and protecting the highest need schools from budget fluctuations
- Developing effective and efficient systems for receiving, processing, tracking, and placing applicants

If the goal of workforce planning and management is to attract qualified individuals into teaching and ensure students' equal access to qualified teachers, state departments are in the best position to implement a systemic approach. Most state data systems in the United States collect information on the number of certified teacher candidates and their certification types, and on attrition and mobility of the teaching workforce. It is possible to identify subject, school type, and location of teacher shortages based on these data. Nevertheless, few states have used these data to develop a systemic approach to addressing teacher shortage and improving teacher quality, because of district and school control of recruitment, hiring, and retention processes. As a result, state efforts have been limited to developing a job bank to facilitate recruitment efforts at districts, and offering incentives in the form of scholarships and loan forgiveness, without focusing on a particular subject or school type (Birman et al., 2007).

In Australia and Japan, improving the overall quality of the teaching workforce and equalizing the distribution of teachers have been the main goals of workforce planning and management. The following sections introduce and discuss recruitment efforts at the state level in Australia and the teacher distribution system in Australia and Japan.

TEACHER RECRUITMENT IN AUSTRALIA

Teacher shortages in mathematics and science in rural and remote locations have been a serious problem in Australia. It also is reported that over the next 10 years, 3.6% of the teaching workforce will reach retirement age each year, which will cause further teacher shortages (MCEETYA, 2005). As mentioned above, the recruitment and hiring of public school teachers are the responsibility of state and territory departments of education. Recruitment programs are well established in most states and territories, and implemented at two stages: (1) recruitment into teacher education programs, and (2) recruitment into teaching. Recruitment policy does not exist in Japan, where there is an oversupply of teacher candidates; therefore, we focus on Australia here. Reviewing recruitment policy programs in Australia provides insight into how the United States can approach recruitment to alleviate the problem of teacher shortage.

Recruitment into Teacher Education Programs

Many states and territories have a recruitment program for high school students and career changers to enter teacher education programs. The state or territory department of education Web site often organizes the information separately for aspiring teachers who are yet to start a teacher education program and teacher candidates who are completing or have completed a teacher education program. Detailed information on what teaching can offer high school students and career changers includes salary and benefits, holiday and leave conditions, incentive programs for individuals who work in rural and remote schools, induction and professional development programs offered in the state or territory, and teacher stories and testaments of how rewarding and meaningful a teaching career can be. Subject areas of teacher shortage are always identified as the areas with the greatest employment opportunities.

Most states and territories offer the most qualified candidates both scholarships that cover the tuition for teacher education programs and guaranteed employment after graduation. These scholarships often are tied to the subject areas of teacher shortage and to rural and remote school locations. For example, the New South Wales Department of Education and Training (2008) offers 230 scholarships yearly to talented aspiring teachers who wish to be employed as secondary teachers in mathematics, science, technological and applied studies, or English, and guaranteed permanent employment in a New South Wales public school in Sydney's western or southwestern suburbs or in a noncoastal rural area of New South Wales.

For career changers, accelerated certification programs and competition-based scholarships are available, especially in the areas of teacher shortage. For example, the Victoria Department of Education and Training (2008b) has a career change program that enables qualified individuals with current industry knowledge and expertise to be trained to become teachers in mathematics and science. Selected career changers receive financial support and paid study leave while they work in the 2-year training program, which combines graduate teacher education courses and supervised classroom duties. Trainees also participate in an induction program in their schools, receiving support from an experienced mentor, and they will be offered an ongoing teaching position after completing the 2-year program. They will be eligible for a retention incentive if they continue to be employed at the appointing school 2 years after the completion of their teacher education course.

In addition to the recruitment programs that target teachers in areas of teacher shortage, many states offer scholarships for Aboriginal and Torres

Strait Islanders to enter into teacher education programs. The objective is to promote diversity and the capacity of the teaching force to address the needs of Aboriginal and Torres Strait Islander students.

Recruitment into the Teaching Profession

Australian state and territory departments of education identify a pool of teacher candidates from three different groups: (1) new graduates of teacher education programs in the state or territory, (2) individuals with teacher certification who have never taught, and (3) teachers from other states or overseas. A state or territory department Web site often has separate sections targeting each of these groups of teacher candidates and explains how to apply for a teaching position along with a list of incentives to become teachers.

The incentives for entering into teaching are offered in four different ways:

1. Special working conditions that include a competitive salary, paid leave and vacations, induction and professional development opportunities, and flexible working hours
2. A graduate recruitment program offering incentives for preservice teachers in the final year of teacher training
3. Incentives for teachers in the subject areas of shortage, such as mathematics, science, and special education
4. Incentives for teachers who work in rural and remote schools

Working conditions and learning opportunities will be addressed in detail in Chapters 4 and 5. Here we focus on the other types of incentives used for recruitment into teaching. A graduate recruitment program is offered in many states and territories to attract teacher candidates into teaching. Since not all students in teacher education programs actually seek employment in teaching, the program aims to encourage all teacher education graduates to pursue teaching careers. The incentives offered by graduate recruitment programs differ from state to state. In New South Wales, for example, many applicants will have interim casual employment to teach in New South Wales public schools by the beginning of term 4 (Australian universities have 4 terms, and term 4 begins around mid-October, with the academic year starting in late January) (New South Wales Department of Education and Training, 2008). In Tasmania, selected graduate recruits will be paid one salary level in advance of first-year salary as an incentive, and they will remain one level above until they reach the top of the salary scale (Tasmania Department of Education, 2008a).

Many incentives are also available for those who plan to teach in subject areas of teacher shortage and in rural and remote areas. The teaching scholarships granted by the Victoria Department of Education and Training (2008d) offer teachers who choose to teach a hard-to-staff subject (identified as mathematics, physics, second language, music, physical education, music, and special education) in a rural or remote school an upfront payment of between A$3,000 and A$5,000 and an additional A$2,000 to A$4,000 after 3 years and 2 months of employment at the school.

Most state and territory departments of education offer a strong incentive plan to attract candidates to work in rural and remote schools with major staffing difficulties. These incentives include: (1) a housing subsidy of 70 to 100%, (2) priority transfer to another school after a certain period of employment, (3) retention benefits of A$5,000 to A$6,000, (4) locality allowances such as climate allowance, vacation travel expenses, and isolation from goods and services allowance, and (5) additional paid leave and/or an additional training and development day.

In addition to these benefits commonly offered to teachers, the Tasmania Department of Education (2008b) offers the Professional Experience in Isolated and Rural Schools program, which supports preservice teachers in undertaking school experience in rural and isolated schools and provides accommodation and travel expenses for the purpose of encouraging teachers to work in these schools after they become certified. Western Australia has a similar program called the Rural Teaching Program, which invites teacher candidates to complete their final practicum in a rural public school. The Rural Teaching Program offers a travel allowance and a weekly stipend ranging from A$120 to A$240, and it further guarantees priority over other graduates for a job in a rural school if a candidate so desires (Western Australia Department of Education and Training, 2008b).

TEACHER HIRING AND DISTRIBUTION
IN AUSTRALIA AND JAPAN

Once a sufficient number of applicants is secured through active recruitment activities, hiring and distribution processes come into play as critical elements in maintaining a high-quality teaching workforce and ensuring an equal distribution of qualified teachers across schools. As explained above, hiring and distribution processes are the responsibility of state and territory departments of education in Australia and prefecture boards of education in Japan. While Japanese prefecture boards of education do not engage in recruitment activities due to the oversupply of teacher candidates, both Australia and Japan have unique hiring and distribution processes that are distinctly different from U.S. practices.

The Hiring Process in Australia

All Australian states and territories have a centralized employment system with a database that stores online application materials from teacher candidates and up-to-date teaching position vacancies in public schools throughout the state or territory. Teacher candidates upload application materials online that typically consist of: (1) proof of registration (certification) that shows the completion of required academic coursework in a teacher education program, (2) official statement of previous service or the most recent practicum report (new graduates only), (3) curriculum vitae, and (4) background information, including citizenship or permanent resident status, criminal background check, and English proficiency. Some states also may request an academic or professional statement and/or referral reports.

In filing application materials, candidates can indicate whether they are open to any position across the state or territory, or indicate that they restrict their choice to a region, a list of schools, or a school in which to be employed. The candidates are informed by the state or territory department of education, however, that they limit their employment possibilities by restricting their choice of region or schools. In either case, vacancy information by school is not available to them, except for those schools that had to advertise as a result of not successfully filling a position through the state or territory human resource department.

Each state or territory department of education's human resource department runs a computerized program in its database to select a candidate based on matched subject area, aptitude, and other expertise for each position. The teachers with priority transfer status (gained after serving in hard-to-staff schools) are given first priority for transfer, followed by other candidates, including those who are guaranteed employment through scholarship programs, those who are returning to teaching after a long-term vacation or study leave, and Aboriginal or Torres Strait Islander candidates. Only after a position has not been filled by these candidates, will other teachers, including new graduates, be considered.

Applicants selected through these state-level screening processes are notified of their candidacy and asked to indicate the intention to pursue an interview or not. If they choose to pursue, they must submit additional materials, such as letters of reference and/or statement of purpose specific to the position. Once the materials are in place, a selection panel will conduct an interview. The members of the selection panel vary by state or territory, but usually include experienced teachers. For example, in Queensland, two to four registered (certified) teachers serve on the selection panel in each of 10 regions or 26 districts across the state (26 districts are divided into 10 regions, and a selection panel may be formed at the region or district level) (Queensland Department of Education, Training and the Arts, 2008). In New South Wales, the panel for a classroom teaching position consists of a principal, teachers, a School Parents and Citizens Association representative, and a representative of the local Aboriginal Education Consultative Group and/or local ethnic community, if applicable (New South Wales Department of Education and Training, 2008).

During the interview, the selection panel may ask questions about the content of the application materials and discuss the applicant's qualifications and prior experiences to clarify the match with the vacant position. An exception to this regular process of initial selection by the state or territory department of education, followed by an interview by a regional selection panel, is some hard-to-staff positions that could not be filled through the centralized employment system. These positions may be advertised through local or interstate newspapers, and teacher candidates can apply directly for the positions and an interview is conducted directly by school personnel. Another exception to these standard hiring processes at the state or territory level is Victoria, where hiring is decentralized and conducted at the school level.

The Hiring Process in Japan

Each prefecture board of education is responsible for hiring teachers within the prefecture in Japan. The hiring process is conducted in two selection stages: (1) a prefectural standardized teacher selection examination and an interview, and (2) a face-to-face exam and an interview. Each board of education administers its own prefecture standardized teacher selection examination, but the content is similar across the prefectures. The teacher selection examination has two components: (1) general knowledge, including philosophy of education, education psychology, education law, history of education, human science, social science, and natural science, and (2) specific subject knowledge (e.g., middle school mathematics, high school science).

The interview at the first selection stage is conducted in 70% of the prefectures, but all prefectures conduct a face-to-face exam and an interview at the second selection stage (MEXT, 2008b). Those who pass the teacher selection examination and interview at the first selection stage are invited to take the face-to-face exam and interview in the second stage. At this stage, over 90% of prefectures use both an individual interview and a group interview, and face-to-face exams may include asking candidates to teach a demonstration lesson or demonstrate lesson plan development (MEXT, 2008b). Criteria for the interview are social and communication skills, commitment to teaching, and overall qualification and capability as a teacher (Nakamoto, 2008). In 2007, 165,251 teacher candidates took the teacher selection examination nationwide, and 22,647 were hired as public school teachers, a success rate of 14% (MEXT, 2008b).

The Distribution Process in Australia

Ensuring equal access to qualified teachers is an important responsibility of education authorities. We have seen that the gap in teacher quality between wealthy and high-poverty schools in Australia is significantly smaller than that in the United States (8.5% vs. 23.1%). State- or territory-wide teacher transfer policies likely explain this small gap.

A teacher distribution process exists in most states and territories for the purpose of ensuring that all schools are equally well staffed. The nature of the distribution process and regional policy varies across the states and territories. In Queensland, for example, all permanent full-time and part-time teachers are required to transfer at some stage under the teacher transfer policy, and they may need to work in a location outside of their preferred locations (Queensland Department of Education, Training and the Arts, 2008). Those who have worked in a location outside of their choice can apply for a transfer to a vacancy in an agreed-upon location after a required period of service—usually about 3 years. Transfer points are calculated based on the number of years served in a hard-to-staff area, mainly rural and remote schools, and accumulated transfer points are used to determine the relative priority of requests for transfer.

However, in most other states, there is no requirement for teachers to transfer, and the distribution process depends on strong incentives to attract qualified candidates to work in hard-to-staff schools in rural and remote schools. Transfer out of these schools after serving a certain period of time—2 to 5 years—is one incentive. While strong incentives ensure staffing in rural and remote schools, interviews with Australian researchers revealed a pattern of new teachers working in rural and remote schools to "do their time" in order to obtain a priority transfer to an urban or suburban location. This transfer system causes a concentration of new teachers in rural and remote schools, and high attrition rates and resulting instability. It is important that strong support be provided to improve working conditions and professional learning opportunities in these schools to encourage the teachers to stay longer.

Despite these limitations, Australian state and territory departments of education have ensured a relatively equal distribution of qualified teachers across the state or territory through these distribution processes. Further analysis of the teacher qualification gap between high-SES and low-SES schools in Australia showed that there is little difference in terms of certification status and subject major between these schools. Australia and the United States share the same challenge of an unequal supply–demand balance based on school location. Australia, however, has established distribution processes to equalize students' access to qualified teachers.

The Distribution Process in Japan

Japan has a more stringent and standardized teacher rotation policy administered by the prefecture boards of education. Rotation policy—*Tenkin*—is a common practice among civil servants and industry, and is widely practiced throughout Japan. Teachers have a standard schedule of rotation where first-year teachers are transferred to another school after about 4 years and other teachers are transferred every 6 years on average.

Initial allocation into a school after being hired as a new teacher also is standardized. Teachers sign a contract that they will work in any school assigned by the prefecture board of education. Human resource officials consider the composition of teachers in each school in terms of the balance of subject areas, age, and gender, and the school size (MEXT, 2007d). Teachers are not free to select a region or a school, yet most teachers seem to accept this as given because this assignment practice is common among all civil servants. Human resources officials also do not perceive a major difference among schools within a prefecture, and are not concerned about the disadvantages or advantages of teachers being placed in one school or another. All teachers go through a prefecture-wide induction program and mentoring system (which will be explained in Chapter 5) and receive a subsidized housing benefit, among other generous benefits; thus, there is no major difference in learning opportunities or housing cost based on location. The small size of each prefecture, compared with an Australian state or U.S. state, may make this stringent policy more acceptable in Japan.

For rotation of practicing teachers, teachers' preference is considered to some extent. In Ibaraki Prefecture, for example, teachers can request a transfer by listing up to four schools of their choice from first to fourth priority. Although a transfer to one of the four schools is not guaranteed, teacher preference is considered by the board of education officials. They also will consult with individual teachers about alternatives if they cannot be transferred into one of the four schools of their choice. Those teachers with special reasons, such as a spouse's employment location and responsibility to take care of an elderly parent in their hometown, are given the first priority to transfer to the schools of their choice.

When the prefecture board of education and MEXT officials were asked the purpose of the teacher rotation policy, most responded that it is for the purposes of allowing rich professional experiences in many locations and revitalization (*Kasseika*) of the teaching workforce within schools. Interestingly, none addressed the equal distribution of qualified teachers among schools. When we consider the stiff competition and stringent selection process, it is understandable that differences in teacher quality may not be a major issue for the board of education officials.

However, this rotation policy results in a distribution of qualified teachers that favors the schools in relatively poor neighborhoods. We have seen in Figure 3.5 that 86.3% of mathematics teachers in low-SES schools are qualified teachers compared with 78.8% in high-SES schools. Whether or not the board of education officials are aware of this figure, Japan has a new teacher allocation policy and teacher rotation policy in place that have resulted in an equitable and needs-based distribution of qualified teachers across schools with different SES levels.

SUMMARY

The eighth-grade mathematics teacher survey data of the TIMSS 2003 show striking national differences in the level of teacher quality and distribution of qualified teachers between wealthy and high-poverty schools in the United States, Australia, and Japan. These differences are explained by recruitment policy and activities in Australia, as well as by hiring and distribution processes in Australia and Japan. While some cultural issues arise in assessing policies that might be viable in the United States, clearly both Australia and Japan have created coherent policies to deal with these issues in a way that the United States simply has not.

Our data show that a smaller percentage of eighth-grade mathematics teachers in the United States are considered qualified than comparable teachers in Japan and eight other high-achieving countries based on the criteria of: (1) full certification, (2) mathematics or mathematics education major, and (3) 3 or more years of teaching experience. This is, paradoxically, good news in that it indicates that one way to improve access to quality teachers is to simply place more effort into recruiting qualified math teachers. However, a major gap in the percentage of qualified teachers between low-SES and high-SES schools also was observed in the United States, and the size of the gap was significantly larger than that in Australia, Japan, and eight other countries. This problem is far less amenable to policy remediation.

An examination of policy and practice in recruitment, hiring, and distribution revealed that a major difference exists in the locus of control: local control versus state control. We pointed out the importance of systemic workforce planning and management in recruiting and hiring the most qualified individuals into teaching, continuously supporting teachers through improving working conditions and professional learning opportunities, and distributing teachers to ensure equal student access to qualified teachers. We focused on recruitment policy and practices in Australia for addressing teacher shortages and improving the quality of the teacher workforce, as well as hiring and distribution policy and practices in Australia and Japan for maximizing student access to qualified teachers.

In reviewing the hiring and distribution policies in Japan and Australia, it is clear that the nature of policies is embedded in the contexts surrounding teachers in each country. The attractiveness of teaching positions in Japan, in comparison with teacher shortages in Australia and the United States, is driven by the social status and privilege given to the teaching profession in Japanese society. The Confucian influence, which highly respects teachers, likely contributes to their high social status in Japan, but national legislation also ensures that teacher salaries are kept relatively high and teachers are given high-quality professional learning opportunities (these will be discussed in Chapters 4 and 5). Thus, teaching is open only to those who excel academically and succeed in the competitive teacher selection examination and interview process. The focus on teacher policy, therefore, is not on recruiting the most qualified, but on selecting the best among qualified candidates.

The distribution policy in Japan is also culturally bound by teachers' views of what it means to be a civil servant. New teacher allocation and teacher rotation policies that allow little room for teacher choice are feasible only in a cultural context where individual teachers are willing to work in any location across the prefecture and do not perceive choice as important. Centrally controlled new teacher allocation and teacher rotation policies are further legitimized by equal funding allocation, centralized induction and professional development opportunities, and subsidized housing and other benefits, which ensure that there are no major differences in working conditions across schools in Japan. Based on the cultural and contextual differences surrounding teachers between Japan and the United States, the hiring and distribution policies in Japan are not likely to be considered for implementation in the United States.

In contrast, Australia has many similarities with the United States in the contexts surrounding teachers. Both countries face teacher shortages in mathematics, science, and special education, among other areas, and there are major regional differences across the country in living conditions and working environments, which caused unbalanced supply–demand dynamics where some districts have an oversupply of teachers while others suffer from major teacher shortages. Australia, however, has taken a systemic approach to recruiting the most qualified individuals into teaching and to distributing them relatively evenly using strong incentives for hard-to-staff regions. This seems to have resulted in a more equitable distribution of qualified teachers between high-SES and low-SES schools than in the United States.

Based on conditions in Australia, we argue that state departments of education are in the best position to engage in systemic workforce planning and management to improve the teacher workforce. Specifically, recruitment, hiring, and distribution processes can be more effective when they are based on a comprehensive understanding of a statewide teacher labor market flow; subject areas and school locations of teacher shortage, and sources of supply through teacher education programs and other alternative routes; and conditions that attract individuals into teaching in hard-to-staff schools.

RECOMMENDATIONS

Based on the comparative analyses of teacher qualifications, the teacher qualification gap, and recruitment, hiring, and distribution policies in the United States, Australia, and Japan, we make the following policy recommendations for improving the quality of the U.S. teacher workforce and equalizing student access to highly qualified teachers.

1. Develop a statewide workforce planning and management system through systematizing recruitment, employment, and distribution processes in collaboration with districts and schools.

A state's capacity to engage in systemic teacher workforce planning and management exceeds that of school districts and schools. Most states have a database that compiles comprehensive data on teachers, including information on certification and coursework in teacher education programs, teacher attrition and transfer, teacher working conditions (including salary), and school demographic and background information. By analyzing teacher attrition and transfer patterns by districts and schools, the state can identify exactly where—by subject areas and district or school locations—a shortage exists. By examining the certification trend by school level (i.e., elementary, middle, or high school) and by subject areas (e.g., mathematics, special education) and the teacher labor market flow from previous years as well as the projection of student enrollment increase, a state can predict where teacher demand will be and develop recruitment strategies to meet the demand for a long time span (4 to 5 years). If a state also collects data on detailed working conditions and teacher induction and professional development, it is possible to identify the predictors of teacher retention and provide support to districts to improve working environments.

Because of its resources and capacity to oversee the teacher labor markets across a state and to address teacher shortages, a state is in the best position to develop a workforce planning and management system that will attract the most qualified individuals into teaching, continuously support them to retain them, and distribute them to equalize student access to qualified teachers. The major inequality in student access to qualified teachers in the United States, which is far more serious than in most other developed countries, provides a strong rationale for the involvement of state departments of education in teacher workforce planning and management. However, because districts and schools play an important role in interviewing and selecting teachers, this system cannot succeed without coordinated efforts and collaboration among a state department of education, districts, and schools.

2. Identify potential teacher candidates other than teacher education graduates and develop recruitment strategies that consider the characteristics of each target population.

In developing recruitment strategies, it is important to target both recruitment into teacher education programs and recruitment into teaching positions. For recruitment into teacher education programs, career changers and high school students are the two major groups. Alternative teacher certification programs have significantly increased the number of teacher candidates across the United States. While continuing state support of alternative teacher education programs, it is also important to attract academically strong high school students into teacher education programs.

Scholarships will be the strongest incentive for these groups, but professional learning opportunities such as state-organized scholarship recipient conferences for developing future leaders and invited participation in decision-making processes in a school district also would be positive incentives for those who are committed to teaching. By targeting, in the awarding of scholarships, those who will pursue certification in subject areas of teacher shortage (e.g., mathematics, science) and who will be willing to work in hard-to-staff schools (e.g., urban or rural areas), it is possible to ensure a supply of qualified teacher candidates in the areas of greatest teacher demand. Guaranteeing employment upon graduation is also possible if a state can work with certain districts with teacher shortages.

For recruitment into teaching positions, in addition to graduates of traditional teacher education programs, it is important to identify two other potential pools of candidates: certified individuals who have never entered teaching, and teachers who left the profession for family reasons. Certified candidates who have never entered into teaching constitute about 42% of all certified individuals (Ingersoll, 2003a). In addition, 13% of those who left teaching during 1999–2000 left for family reasons, mostly likely marriage and child-rearing responsibility (Provasnik & Dorfman, 2005).

Recruiting efforts toward certified individuals who have never entered teaching can emphasize the opportunity to apply their professional experience to teaching, the rewarding experience of working with children and adolescents, systemic induction and professional learning programs, and financial incentives (e.g., bonus, longer paid leave) to work in hard-to-staff schools. For teachers who left teaching for family reasons, recruitment efforts can emphasize flexible working hours, subsidy for day care or babysitting, extra funds for professional development to update teaching skills and knowledge, and financial incentives to work in hard-to-staff schools.

In addition to posting the recruitment efforts that target each of these different pools of potential teacher candidates on their Web sites, state departments of education can broadcast on TV and advertise in newspapers. As the departments maintain a teacher database of those who are certified and who have left teaching, a postcard describing the benefits of seeking a teaching position, along with an incentive plan, can be sent to these individuals. Recruitment becomes more effective when the application process is streamlined at the state level and an applicant needs to simply upload required materials once.

3. Streamline the hiring process at state and district levels, with strong incentives to work in hard-to-staff schools.

By centralizing the application and initial selection processes at the state level and conducting final selection through interviews at the school district level, the hiring process can be streamlined systematically. The use of a centralized database with standardized application materials allows candidates to upload one application to apply for multiple positions. Having a list of all available positions across the state, along with information on the incentive package for working in hard-to-staff schools, helps candidates make informed decisions as to which districts to apply to. Candidates can be given an option to select a school, multiple schools, a district, or multiple districts that they want their applications to target. This will increase candidates' employment opportunities in an efficient application process that requires little time.

School districts also benefit from reducing the cost and time for posting advertisements and reviewing application materials. The state computerized database can quickly compile a list of matched candidates in terms of school and grade level, subject areas, and required experience from a pool of candidates. A school district then can review the list and invite candidates for an interview once they have agreed to be considered for the position. This process can be done throughout the academic year, with districts posting advertisements for open positions on the state department Web site and the department providing matched candidates for the positions to the school districts as soon as they are available.

This process requires effective collaboration and a trusting relationship between school districts and the state departments of education for establishing standardized application requirements and materials, and selection criteria that meet the needs of school districts. It may have to start with voluntary participation of school districts to test how it works. Once it is established, however, the application process becomes efficient, while candidates are better informed about job availability across the state and incentives for working in hard-to-staff schools. An efficient application and selection process is an important factor in attracting qualified candidates into the teaching profession. This streamlined hiring process solves the problems of late hiring in large urban districts by expediting the selection of candidates based on database matching of qualifications. Most important, this centralized hiring process helps the state engage in systemic workforce management by distributing qualified candidates across the state and alleviating teacher shortages in hard-to-staff schools through a strong incentive plan.

4. Monitor the balance of qualified teachers among schools, and use incentives to equalize student access to qualified teachers.

The state departments of education can continuously monitor the balance of qualified teachers across schools. When there is a major imbalance, such as a concentration of inexperienced teachers or uncertified teachers, they can use strong incentives to encourage qualified teachers to transfer to schools with a fewer number of qualified teachers. The incentives can include a salary increase, one-time bonus, extra paid leave, extra release time and funds for professional development, and subsidized housing and commuting expenses.

If the state can work with hard-to-staff districts, it may be able to institute a transfer program where qualified teachers commit to work there for 3 to 5 years, with further incentives provided if they stay longer than the contracted period. It is important, however, that this process not cause high attrition and instability in hard-to-staff schools, as is happening in Australia. Stronger support for these teachers through extended mentoring, professional development opportunities, and improved working conditions, as well as strong leadership and support from principals, is critical for these teachers to stay longer in these schools. When this type of transfer process is practiced, along with recruiting efforts targeting individuals in subject areas of teacher shortage and individuals who are willing to work in hard-to-staff districts, the major teacher quality gap that has existed for so many years is likely to be narrowed, and all U.S. students will have equal access to qualified teachers—the most important education right of all students around the world.

Teachers' Working Conditions

WORKING CONDITIONS influence teacher motivation, commitment, job performance, and productivity (Johnson, 2006; Johnson & Project on the Next Generation of Teachers, 2004). Working conditions also play a significant role in teacher attrition and retention (Bonesronning, Falch, & Strom, 2005; Hanushek, Kain, & Rivkin, 2004; Marvel, Lyter, Peltola, Strizek, & Morton, 2006).When teachers are assigned too many classes to teach, must teach multiple subject areas outside of their expertise, or are given inadequate preparation periods, they cannot be expected to deliver high-quality instruction. Teacher pay (which we consider part of working conditions) also is an important factor, drawing qualified individuals into other occupations (Clotfelter, Glennie, Ladd, & Vigdor, 2006; Hanushek et al., 2004) or forcing teachers to take supplemental jobs in order to make ends meet. Thus managing teacher working conditions in order to promote teacher professionalism, confidence and pride, and work performance is a major responsibility of educational policymakers and administrators around the world.

In this chapter, we focus on two major dimensions of working conditions: (1) workload and assignment, and (2) compensation and benefits. We look at the United States, Australia, Japan, and 12 other high-achieving countries, using teacher survey data from the TIMSS 2003 data set, OECD data, and policy documents on teachers' working conditions. These two dimensions of working conditions were chosen because they are relatively amenable to change through policy intervention, as opposed to equally critical dimensions such as school climate or cultural perceptions of teaching, which are relatively resistant to reform. Also, teaching loads and compensation are dimensions that are readily comparable among developed nations. Even factors such as class size and use of specific instructional materials (e.g., computers) tend to be more conditioned by national cultural differences than are these two dimensions.

For workload and assignments, we examine four indicators of working conditions: (1) instructional workload, (2) multiple-subject teaching assignment, (3) out-of-field teaching, and (4) noninstructional workload.

For compensation and benefits, we compare three indicators: (1) salary, (2) allowances, and (3) leave. Again, these indicators are relatively standard among developed nations, although they may vary greatly among developing nations. Our focus is on viable policy solutions that can be applied in the U.S. context.

WORKLOAD AND ASSIGNMENT

Instructional Workload

In the TIMSS survey, eighth-grade mathematics teachers around the world were asked a set of questions about their instructional workload. They first were asked, "In one typical calender week from Monday to Friday, what is the total number of single periods for which you are formally scheduled?" Then they were asked, "Of these formally scheduled periods, how many are you assigned to: (1) teach mathematics, (2) teach science, and (3) teach other subjects." Based on an additional question— "How many minutes are in a typical single period?"—we computed the formal instructional workload for math, science, and other subjects. We added the number of teaching periods, multiplied by the minutes in a single period, and divided by 60 to compute the hours per week formally scheduled for instruction. This computation allowed standardization across countries, as there is some variation in period length. The computation does not take into account classes that teachers might pick up informally—say, if a colleague was out sick. The estimates of instructional time are therefore conservative.

Instruction is the main part of the teacher's job, but not the only part. Without going into issues of teacher work in administration, guidance, or other forms of nonacademic supervision (see LeTendre, Baker, Akiba, & Wiseman, 2001b), teachers often have a good deal of academic-related work that they do outside of the school day. Mathematics teachers were also asked, "Outside the formal school day, approximately how many hours per week do you normally spend on each of these activities: (1) grading student tests, exams, or other student work, and (2) planning lessons?" The numbers of hours spent on this at-school instruction and outside-school grading and lesson planning are shown in Figure 4.1.

This combined instructional workload gives a good estimate of the time teachers concentrate on instruction and academic-related work. The average of the combined 12 high-achieving countries is 30.0 hours, followed by the United States (28.3 hours), Australia (25.8 hours), and Japan (23.1 hours). As we will discuss later, these numbers suggest that even in the

Figure 4.1. Teacher workload: At-school and outside-school instructional tasks.

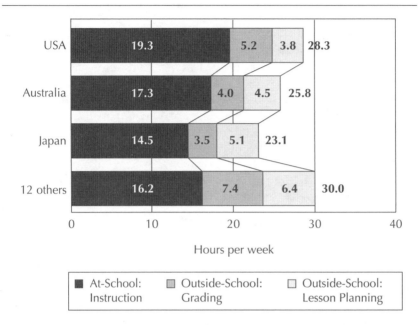

Hours per week

■ At-School: ▨ Outside-School: ☐ Outside-School:
   Instruction   Grading   Lesson Planning

Notes: "12 others" indicates average percentage of Belgium (Flemish), Estonia, Hong Kong, Hungary, Latvia, Malaysia, the Netherlands, the Russian Federation, Singapore, the Slovak Republic, South Korea, and Taiwan. All figures in this chapter from TIMSS database.

highest scoring countries, a substantial portion of teachers' work is taken up by a range of other activities—administrative duties, meeting with other teachers, meeting with students, and meeting with parents.

However, if we look only at the time formally allotted for instruction, we see that U.S. teachers are assigned to teach the longest hours (19.6) of any of the nations in this sample. U.S. teachers have substantially more instructional hours per week than their Japanese peers (14.5) or even than their Australian counterparts (17.3). Surprisingly, the average of the 12 other countries is only 16.2 hours, suggesting that U.S. mathematics teachers' average of 4 formal instructional hours each day is among the highest in the developed world.

For outside-school instructional tasks, the cross-national pattern is complicated, with Japanese teachers spending more time on lesson planning than on grading, in contrast to U.S. teachers and teachers in 12 other countries, who spend more time on grading than on lesson planning. In

Australia, teachers spend about the same amount of time on grading and lesson planning. While grading is important for assessing the level of student understanding of course materials, the small amount of time spent on lesson planning among U.S. teachers is alarming, considering the heavy teaching load. The ratio of teaching hours to lesson planning hours is 5.1 (19.3/3.8) in the United States, which means that U.S. teachers spend 1 hour on preparation for 5 hours of lessons. That ratio is larger than in Australia (3.8), Japan (2.8), and 12 other countries (2.5). Although more lesson-planning hours do not necessary equate with quality instruction, it is unlikely that U.S. teachers feel they are delivering well-prepared lessons when they spend only 3.8 hours per week planning lessons for 19.6 hours of teaching. Previous studies of Japanese instructional practices explicitly linked extensive planning with improved lesson quality and instructional quality (Fernandez & Yoshida, 2004; Lewis & Tsuchida, 1998; Linn, Lewis, Tsuchida, & Songer, 2000).

Multiple-Subject Assignment

When teachers are assigned to teach multiple subject areas, it typically requires greater amounts of preparation time and effort. "Out-of-field" teaching has been identified as one of the most likely causes of poor lesson planning, poor instructional quality, and thus lower student achievement (Ingersoll, 1996). As most eighth-grade teachers around the world are not prepared to specialize in multiple subject areas, being assigned multiple subject areas to teach typically requires a greater expenditure of energy. There also may be more stress associated with teaching unfamiliar subject areas. Figure 4.2 presents the hours of teaching by subject areas assigned to mathematics teachers.

As we would expect, math teachers do spend the majority of their time teaching mathematics. However, the amount of time allocated to teaching other subjects areas varies across nations. In Australia, mathematics teachers spend 4.4 hours per week teaching either science or other subject areas, significantly higher than in the United States (2.7 hours), Japan (1.6 hours), and 12 other countries (3.3 hours on average). About 25% of the formal teaching load of Australian math teachers is in subjects other than math, in contrast to U.S. teachers (14.0%), Japanese teachers (11.0%), and teachers in 12 other countries (20.3% on average).

These statistics show an important result of how teaching assignments are managed in each country. When school administrators cannot fill a position in certain subject areas, they may assign other teachers to teach the subject areas. In an Australian national survey of beginning teachers with 3 or fewer years of teaching experience, 44% of teachers indeed re-

Figure 4.2. Multiple-subject teaching load.

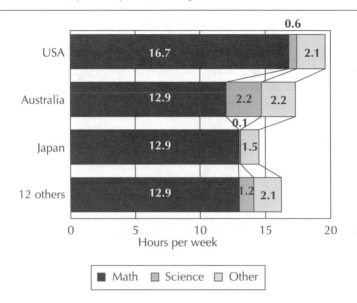

Note: "12 others" indicates average percentage of Belgium (Flemish), Estonia, Hong Kong, Hungary, Latvia, Malaysia, the Netherlands, the Russian Federation, Singapore, the Slovak Republic, South Korea, and Taiwan.

ported that they had been asked to teach outside their area of expertise or qualification (Australian Education Union, 2006). However, Australian teacher education programs encourage teacher candidates to specialize in two subject areas to maximize their employment opportunities. Also, re-training opportunities are offered through many state and territory depart-ments of education in fields of shortage, such as mathematics, science, and technology. While this may be an efficient way to address teacher short-age, it is important to consider the workload and the stress that teaching multiple subject areas could cause teachers. Given the in-depth content knowledge required to teach each subject area at the secondary school level, it would be difficult to expect teachers to be as effective in teaching multiple subject areas as in focusing on a single subject area.

Out-of-Field Teaching

Out-of-field teaching is another barrier to effective teaching, yet it is widely practiced in many countries suffering from teacher shortage (Australian

Education Union, 2006; Ingersoll, 1999, 2001). Earlier we discussed the problems that math teachers face when they have to teach a subject other than mathematics. Those instances, however, pale in comparison to the data below, which address the issue of whether or not teachers of mathematics actually have been trained to teach math. When teachers without a mathematics or mathematics education major teach mathematics, they have limited content knowledge and are less likely to teach effectively. Figure 4.3 shows the percentage of mathematics teachers without a mathematics or mathematics education major. As out-of-field teaching is likely to differ between low-SES and high-SES schools with different levels of teacher shortage (Ingersoll, 2002; Jerald & Ingersoll, 2002), the graph is shown separately for low-SES (bottom one-third) and high-SES schools (top one-third).

Out-of-field teaching is shockingly prevalent in the United States; nearly a third (29.7%) of teachers sampled in the TIMSS survey are teaching mathematics without an undergraduate degree in mathematics or even

Figure 4.3. Out-of-field teaching by school SES level.

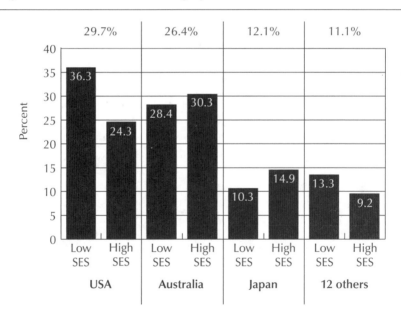

Note: "12 others" indicates average percentage of Belgium (Flemish), Estonia, Hong Kong, Hungary, Latvia, Malaysia, the Netherlands, the Russian Federation, Singapore, the Slovak Republic, South Korea, and Taiwan.

a mathematics education major. Australia also suffers from high rates of out-of-field teaching, albeit at a slightly lower percentage than in the United States. Over a quarter (26.4%) are teaching without a mathematics or mathematics education major. The percentage is significantly lower in Japan and 12 other countries; only 12.1% and 11.1%, respectively, are teaching without a subject major degree.

These numbers are alarming enough—the differences between the United States and top-performing nations do not have to be gleaned from advanced statistical calculations of significance, but can be seen readily in terms of simple percentages. When we consider differential student access, the numbers are even more shocking. The difference between low-SES and high-SES students is most pronounced in the United States. There is a major gap—12.0%—in the percentage of teachers teaching mathematics without a mathematics major or mathematics education major by the level of mean socioeconomic status (36.4% in low-SES schools vs. 24.3% in high-SES schools). The difference is only 4.1% (13.3 vs. 9.2) in the average of 12 other countries. The United States is clearly out of line with global norms in terms of giving poor children access to teachers with a subject major.

If we compare the United States with Australia and Japan, we see not only lower rates of out-of-field teaching, but the results of systems that actively work to reduce educational inequality. In both of these nations, low-SES schools have a smaller percentage of out-of-field teachers than high-SES schools. In Australia, 28.4% of mathematics teachers in low-SES schools are out-of-field teachers, compared with 30.3% in high-SES schools. In Japan, the percentages are 10.3 in low-SES schools and 14.9 in high-SES schools. U.S. teachers, however, are more likely to be assigned to teach out-of-field subjects when they work in low-SES schools than when they work in high-SES schools. This difference in a critical aspect of working conditions is likely to discourage qualified teachers from working in low-SES schools. In contrast, Australian and Japanese teachers are not disadvantaged in being assigned out-of-field subjects when they work in low-SES schools. Indeed, their chances of being assigned out-of-field subjects are lower in low-SES schools than in high-SES schools. This working condition can be an incentive for teachers to work in low-SES schools.

While the prevalence of out-of-field teaching in low-SES schools in the United States is likely the result of greater teacher shortages in these schools (particularly in math), it is important to note that this situation does not exist in Australia, even though there is large problem overall with out-of-field math teaching. Also, although Australia is a large nation and faces significant issues in terms of staffing remote rural areas, it has succeeded in

preventing an imbalance that is likely to adversely affect the most economically disadvantaged. This is likely the result of the efficient centralized hiring system and the active recruitment of qualified teachers into
rural and remote schools using attractive incentives (see Chapter 3). A
smaller gap in overall teacher quality between low-SES and high-SES
schools in Australia than in the United States, as shown in Figure 3.5,
means that there is less pressure on school administrators to assign teachers to teach out-of-field subjects.

Noninstructional Workload

Teachers' responsibilities are not limited to instruction. They need to su-
pervise students during lunch, club activities, and various school events;
communicate with and visit students' families and community members;
and attend faculty meetings and professional development activities,
among other things. In addition, there are many administrative and record-
keeping tasks that can take a great amount of time.

To understand the amount of noninstructional workload, we computed
the average number of hours teachers spend per week on noninstructional
tasks. Eighth-grade mathematics teachers were asked how many periods in a typical calendar week they were assigned to perform duties other
than teaching, and the number of periods was converted into hours per
week. They also were asked approximately how many hours per week
outside the formal school day they spent on (1) administrative and record-
keeping tasks, including staff meetings, and (2) other tasks (other than
grading and lesson planning). These two items were added to create the
total number of hours for noninstructional tasks outside school. Figure 4.4
shows the number of hours teachers spent on noninstructional tasks at
school and outside school.

U.S. teachers reported the largest number of hours spent on noninstructional tasks at school: 2.4 hours per week compared with only 1.4
hours in Australia, 1.5 hours in Japan, and 0.7 hour in 12 other countries. In all the countries, however, teachers reported a greater number
of hours spent on noninstructional tasks outside school. Japanese teachers
reported a significantly greater number of hours—11.5 per week—than
teachers in 12 other countries (6.2), Australian teachers (6.0), and U.S.
teachers (4.5).

The greater amount of time spent on noninstructional tasks outside
school than at school in all the countries indicates that the formally scheduled hours are not sufficient to complete the required tasks to fulfill teachers' responsibilities. Teachers typically are not paid for outside-school
work, and this informal workload can place stress on teachers. The heavy

Figure 4.4. Teacher workload: At-school and outside-school noninstructional tasks.

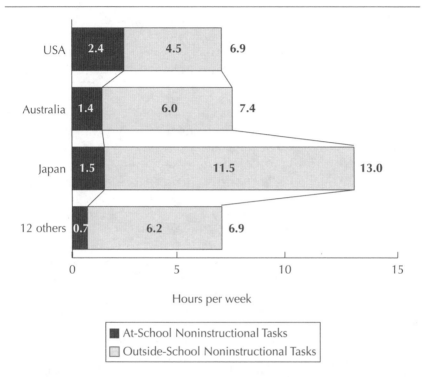

Hours per week

■ At-School Noninstructional Tasks
☐ Outside-School Noninstructional Tasks

Note: "12 others" indicates average percentage of Belgium (Flemish), Estonia, Hong Kong, Hungary, Latvia, Malaysia, the Netherlands, the Russian Federation, Singapore, the Slovak Republic, South Korea, and Taiwan.

outside-school workload among Japanese teachers can be explained by the fact that many of them need to spend a great amount of time supervising club activities before and after school as well as on weekends. Our previous work has shown that the multiple responsibilities of Japanese teachers include teaching, student counseling, visiting families, and club activities and various school events for promoting academic, social, psychological, and physical development (LeTendre, 1994, 1995, 2000; LeTendre & Akiba, 2001). The focus on whole-person education also was expressed in the vision of high-quality teachers, as we saw in Chapter 2. These multiple responsibilities, however, could lead to serious stress and burnout of teachers. According to a national survey in Japan, 61% of middle school teachers reported that they are busy all the time, and the number of teachers who took leave for a mental health reason has increased dramatically from 1,240 in 1995 to 3,559 in 2004 (Shimizu et al., 2006).

When we combine both instructional and noninstructional tasks outside regular school hours from Figures 4.1 and 4.4, we see that the greatest number of hours was spent by Japanese teachers, 20.1 hours per week outside school, followed by 12 other countries (20 hours), Australia (14.5 hours), and the United States (13.5 hours). U.S. and Australian teachers spend less time outside school on school-related work than teachers in other high-achieving countries. Even so, they spend close to 3 hours each day working outside school. While this amount of overtime work may be common in many professions, it becomes a problem especially when teachers are not paid well compared with other professions and not compensated for the extra hours they put into schoolwork.

COMPENSATION AND BENEFITS

Salary

Teacher salary has long been a focus of debate in the United States. According to the American Federation of Teachers' (2007) report, in 2005 teachers on average earned $16,000 less than 23 other professions requiring a college degree, as identified by the Bureau of Labor Statistics, and the gap has grown over the past 5 years. In addition, the average salary increase between 2003–04 and 2004–05 was 2.2%, which is lower than the 3.4% increase in the cost of living shown in the Consumer Price Index (American Federation of Teachers, 2007). These statistics indicate that teaching is not a financially attractive profession compared with other professions, and it has become increasingly less so in recent years.

How does U.S. teachers' salary compare with that of other countries? Figure 4.5 shows the average teacher salary in lower secondary education at the starting point (new teachers) and after 15 years of service in U.S. dollars in the United States, Australia, and Japan, obtained from OECD (2007) statistics. First-year U.S. teachers earned an average of US$32,225, which was higher than US$31,092 in Australia and US$25,593 in Japan. However, a salary gap emerges after 15 years of teaching. U.S. teachers earned an average of US$41,090, lower than US$44,526 in Australia and US$47,855 in Japan. The gap between the United States and Japan is over US$10,000 a year.

The increase from the starting point to after 15 years of service shows the financial prospect in the teaching profession. The small increase in U.S.

Figure 4.5. Teacher salary at the starting point and after 15 years (2000 U.S. dollars).

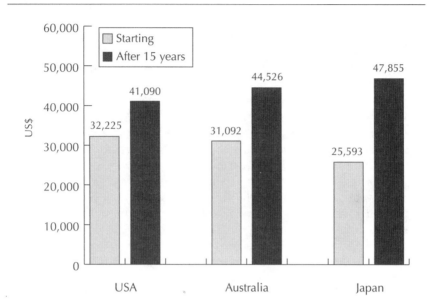

Source: (OECD, 2007).

teachers' salary over a 15-year span discourages qualified candidates from pursuing teaching. It also discourages practicing teachers from staying in the profession. Especially in areas of high needs, such as mathematics and science, it is no surprise that teacher candidates and practicing teachers consider seeking a more financially rewarding job. Among mathematics and science teachers who left teaching during 2004–05, 25.3% listed "better salary or benefits" as an important reason, the second most prominent reason after retirement, according to national statistics (Hampden-Thompson, Herring, & Kienzl, 2008).

Another way to look at teacher salary is through a comparison with GDP per capita. GDP per capita is defined as the total market value of all final goods and services produced within a given country in a calendar year divided by the population, and it is an indicator of the country's economic wealth per capita. The ratio of teacher salary to GDP per capita can show the standing of teachers' salary relative to the country's economic wealth. The ratio of teacher salary after 15 years to GDP per capita is 0.98 in the United States, 1.30 in Australia, and 1.56 in Japan (OECD, 2007). While Australian and Japanese teachers are paid 1.3 and 1.56 times GDP per capita, U.S. teachers are paid about the same as GDP per capita. This statistic also indicates that in both Australia and Japan, teaching is likely to be regarded as above average or of higher status because teachers make more than the average worker.

Taken together, these statistics show that U.S. teachers are not paid as well as Australian or Japanese teachers, and there is a major gap in salary after 15 years of teaching between the United States and Japan. While Australian teachers with 15 years of service earn $3,436 more than U.S. teachers, teacher salary is debated as a major problem in Australia as well. According to a national survey conducted by the Australian Education Union (AEU) (2006), 56% of beginning teachers with 3 or fewer years of service reported that teacher salary is a major concern, the third most common concern after workload (64%) and behavior management (60%). The AEU has played an important role in improving teachers' salary, especially in recent years. For example, the AEU Victorian Branch (2008) recently achieved a government agreement to increase starting teacher salary to A$51,184 and the top of the salary scale to A$75,500. These amounts will increase to A$55,459 and A$81,806, respectively, by 2011.

In Japan, teacher salary is not considered a problem as it is protected by the Education Personnel Quality Assurance Law. During the time of rapid economic growth in the 1960s, Japan faced losing qualified teacher candidates to other professions with a better salary. To attract qualified individuals into the teaching profession, the Education Personnel Quality Assurance Law was established in 1974, which required the prefecture boards of education to keep teacher salary higher than that of other civil servants (Central Education Committee, 2007). As a result, a greater number of teacher candidates has started to take the teacher selection exams, and only a small percentage of the most qualified candidates are hired as teachers (Central Education Committee, 2007).

Allowances

Various types of allowances are another important source of income that reduces the financial burden associated with housing, travel, teaching materials, and professional development activities. The nature and type of allowances differ among the United States, Australia, and Japan. In addition, the level of standardization in allowances varies significantly. While in the United States, teacher allowances are determined by school districts or states, in Australia they are determined by state and territory departments of education, which are the employers of public school teachers. In Japan, teacher allowances are standardized across the country and determined by the Ministry of Education.

In the United States, tuition reimbursement is most commonly offered by school districts or states (National Council on Teacher Quality, 2006). Teachers are reimbursed up to a certain number of credit hours or up to a certain amount of funds. This serves as an incentive for teachers to earn advanced degrees, which leads them to a higher salary scale. Teachers also may take university courses for professional development purposes. Many districts also provide funds for professional development activities for individual teachers. There are major variations in the type and amount of allowances given to teachers across school districts due to the differing educational funds available. There is no national or state report to date that examines the variation and types of teacher allowances across school districts.

In Australia, teacher allowances are determined by the state or territory department of education and are applied consistently across the state or territory. Housing subsidies commonly are provided to teachers who work in remote areas where there is a shortage of satisfactory rental housing. In New South Wales, for example, the Teacher Housing Authority maintains a number of houses and villa units throughout the state, and 70 to 90% of rent is subsidized for teachers in remote areas (New South Wales Department of Education and Training, 2008). In the Northern Territory, in addition to receiving free housing in remote areas, teachers are provided with up to A\$1,819 a year as a professional isolation allowance for attending conferences and courses, buying professional resources, and facilitating on-site professional development (Northern Territory Government, 2008). Furthermore, they are given up to three airfares out of an isolated locality for themselves and dependents for personal reasons. Queensland and Western Australia have a similar program for teachers in remote areas.

These allowances are provided as incentives for teachers to work in remote areas. Other allowances applicable to all teachers include an extra allowance for working overtime, a meal allowance for working at school past dinner time, and an allowance for supervising preservice teachers. In addition to these allowances, Victoria has a higher duties allowance and special payments (Victoria Department of Education and Training, 2008a). A higher duties allowance is given to a teacher assigned to a responsibility or particular task of another position with a higher salary scale. The teacher is paid 91.7% of the difference between the current salary and the minimum salary of the assigned position for a period ranging from 1 week to 12 months. A special payment is provided to a teacher who is assigned a task in addition to the responsibilities of his or her position. Special payments vary from A\$500 to A\$6,000 per task based on the length and nature of the assigned tasks. Special payments can be granted for between

3 months and 2 years. The Victorian Government Schools Agreement 2004 and the Victorian Government Schools–School Services Officers Agreement 2004 specified that special payments can be used for attracting or retaining teachers as well. Considering that many teachers are taking on extra duties, especially in schools with teacher shortages, these programs can be good incentives for teacher recruitment and retention.

In Japan, teacher allowances are standardized and specified by the Ministry of Education. The main allowance programs are the educational personnel adjustment allowance, which provides 4% of the teacher salary to all teachers to cover overtime work, and the teacher special allowance, which provides an additional 7% of the individual teacher salary to all teachers. This standardized allocation method has been criticized based on recent national survey results showing a major variation in the amount of overtime work among teachers, ranging from none to more than 5 hours a day (MEXT, 2007).

The Central Education Committee appointed by the Ministry of Education recently recommended that the prefecture boards of education abolish or reduce the teacher special allowance and use the funds for performance-based pay or other allowances (Central Education Committee, 2007). However, a national survey showed that Japanese teachers are not supportive of performance-based teacher salary (MEXT, 2006). As a result, very few prefectures to date have used a performance-based salary scheme. As an alternative to differential salary, the Expert Teacher System, a career ladder system with an increased number of positions with different salary scales, was proposed to reward high-quality teachers and is being implemented increasingly across the country. As of 2006, 18% of prefectures had implemented this system, which gives a leadership position and higher salary to high-quality teachers, and 47% were preparing for its implementation.

The other available teacher allowances in Japan are for club activities, supervision of students at sports competitions and standardized exams, and school trips (Central Education Committee, 2007). The amount of these allowances is minimal and rarely exceeds US$1,000 a year for the sum of these allowances. In addition to these allowances provided by the Ministry, teachers also receive housing subsidies and housing mortgages with special low interest rates from teacher unions. For example, teachers can receive up to US$270 a month for housing rental from the Ibaraki Prefecture Teacher Union (2007). There are also teacher housing units, depending on the region, for which teachers pay only US$20 to US$40 a month. When teachers purchase a house, they are entitled to an interest rate of 2.26%, significantly lower than the average mortgage interest rate in Japan. These generous allowances are considered privileges of the teaching profession and serve as strong incentives for attracting teacher candidates and maintaining high retention rates.

Leave

Leave is an important benefit given to teachers, who are constantly overworked. In addition to regular sick and personal leave, extended parental leave for the birth or adoption of a child enhances the retention rates of teachers as they do not need to quit teaching for child rearing. In addition, sabbatical or study leave enhances teachers' opportunities for professional learning, which is an important working condition that supports teacher professionalism.

In examining the types and length of leave, it is important to consider the length of teacher contracts. In the United States, a teacher contract generally covers between 9 and 10 months a year aligned with the school academic year, which means that teachers are granted 2 to 3 months of unpaid release from work per year. If teachers choose to teach in summer school, they are paid extra for the period of service outside their contract. In Australia and Japan, the contract is for 12 months. The academic year runs for 9 to 10 months in Australia, and teachers are granted a long period of paid vacation leave of 1 to 2 months. The academic year in Japan, however, runs for 11 months and teachers are given only 20 days of paid leave per year.

U.S. teachers are granted an average of 10 to 15 days of sick and personal leave during their contract period. Family leave for the birth or adoption of a child is about 12 weeks, but teachers are not paid during this period (American Federation of Teachers, 2002). While teachers may be able to use paid sick or personal leave as part of family leave, depending on the district and state, family leave can create financial strain. This short period of family leave without pay makes it difficult for female teachers to remain in teaching. A national survey showed that, during 2004–05, 19% of teachers who left teaching reported that pregnancy or child rearing was a very or extremely important reason (Marvel, Lyter, Peltola, Strizek, & Morton, 2006).

Family leave in Australia and Japan is significantly longer, and teachers are partially paid during the leave. Family leave in Australia differs by state or territory, but most states and territories grant 52 weeks of family leave, with paid leave ranging from 6 weeks (e.g., South Australia) to 14 weeks (e.g., Northern Territory, Victoria, and Western Australia). In the Northern Territory, teachers can accrue up to 6 years of unpaid family leave, and in Victoria, teachers can extend family leave up to the 7th birthday of the child. These conditions for family leave make it easier for teachers to come back to work and remain in the teaching profession after completing a family leave. In Japan, every female teacher across the country can take up to 3 years of maternity leave per child, and 50% of the teacher salary is paid during the first 12 months. Many teachers return to teaching after taking a maternity leave due to the sufficient length of the leave.

Another important leave is sabbatical or study leave. While sabbatical or study leave is commonly available to Australian and Japanese teachers, it is rarely offered to U.S. teachers. Several Australian states offer sabbatical leave with a deferred salary scheme. In New South Wales, for example, teachers have an option to defer 20% of their salary for the first 4 years and take 1 year off with the deferred salary for the purposes of professional development and renewal experiences such as postgraduate study, working in overseas education systems, and other professional activities (New South Wales Department of Education and Training, 2008). In Victoria, teachers can take sabbatical leave with a similar deferred salary scheme for up to 4 years as long as their term of employment prior to the leave is at least as long as the sabbatical leave period (Victoria Department of Education and Training, 2008c).

Some states also offer a paid long service leave for teachers who have completed a certain period of service. In Western Australia, 13 weeks of paid long service leave are granted after 10 years of service and after every additional 7 years of continuous service (Western Australia Department of Education and Training, 2008a). In New South Wales, teachers are granted 8 weeks of paid leave after 10 years of service, and for each additional year, they are given 15 days of paid leave (New South Wales Department of Education and Training, 2003).

Study leave is granted to Australian teachers who take courses that are highly relevant to their professional development or of particular value to the state or territory department. In New South Wales, teachers are eligible to apply for a study leave after 2 years of continuous service (New South Wales Department of Education and Training, 2003). Teachers can apply for scholarships and competitive or noncompetitive awards offered by the department to cover tuition and a stipend. After they return to teaching, they are required to serve twice as long a period as the study leave period; for example, a teacher who took a 1-year leave would be required to teach 2 years after the leave. In the Northern Territory, teachers living in remote localities are eligible for one semester of paid study leave or two semesters at half pay (Northern Territory Government, 2008).

Study leave is also available to Japanese teachers who seek an advanced teacher certificate or degree at a graduate school (MEXT, 2008b). Teachers who have served at least 3 years are eligible to apply for a study leave of 1 to 3 years. They generally are not paid during the leave, but they also can apply for a paid leave on a competitive basis. They can study at a graduate school either in Japan or abroad to pursue a higher degree or seek an advanced teacher certificate. This serves as a good incentive for teachers to pursue further study for professional development.

SUMMARY

Comparisons of the statistics on workload, assignment, and salary, and examinations of policy documents on teacher allowances and leave have shown the different conditions teachers work under in the United States, Australia, and Japan. Are U.S. teachers' working conditions better than those of Australian and Japanese teachers? The answer depends on which dimension of working conditions we focus on.

U.S. teachers are assigned to teach longer hours (19.6 hours per week) than Australian teachers (17.3) and Japanese teachers (14.5), and the average of 12 other countries (16.2). Yet, they spend the least amount of time preparing lessons among all the countries, and spend more time grading exams, tests, and student work than teachers in Australia and Japan. This may be a result of U.S. teachers focusing on teaching procedural skills using worksheets in class more often than other teachers (Hiebert et al., 2005). Also, our previous work found that U.S. mathematics teachers assign more homework than Australian and Japanese teachers: 140 minutes of homework per week compared with 100 minutes in Australia and 70 minutes in Japan (LeTendre & Akiba, 2005).

Since U.S. teachers spend a small amount of time on lesson planning, we cannot expect them to deliver a well-prepared lesson that focuses on conceptual understanding and higher order thinking. It is likely that U.S. teachers are left with less time for preparing lessons because they are given heavier teaching loads than Australian or Japanese teachers. U.S. teachers spend 28.6 hours per week—a greater amount of total time for instruction, grading, and lesson planning combined together than Australian teachers (25.8 hours) and Japanese teachers (23.1 hours). Because they spend unpaid, unscheduled hours on grading and lesson planning, it is natural for them to orient their lessons so that less time is required for preparation—the lessons on procedural skills using worksheets and greater amounts of homework. This may be the only way to manage teaching 4 hours of lessons each day on top of other noninstructional duties. U.S. teachers' work schedule needs to be improved to allow them sufficient time for lesson planning.

A comparison of multiple-subject teaching showed that Australian mathematics teachers are most likely to be assigned to teach multiple subject areas. On average, mathematics teachers spend 25% of their time teaching other subjects in Australia, compared with 14.0% in the United States, 11.0% in Japan, and 20.3% in 12 other countries. This multiple-subject teaching responsibility of Australian teachers needs to be reconsidered in light of the workload and the stress it could cause them. U.S. teachers' degree of multiple-subject responsibility is less than that in Australia; in both countries, however, many mathematics teachers do not possess a mathematics major or mathematics education major.

A comparison of out-of-field teaching measured by the percentage of teachers teaching mathematics without a major in mathematics or mathematics education showed that out-of-field teaching is more prevalent in the United States than in other countries. About one third of U.S. teachers are out-of-field teachers (29.7%) compared with 26.4% in Australia, 12.1% percent in Japan, and 11.1% in 12 other high-achieving countries. Such U.S. out-of-field teaching is especially prevalent in low-SES schools, where 36.3% of mathematics teachers do not have a major in mathematics or mathematics education, compared with 24.3% in high-SES schools.

This gap explains the major difference in working conditions between low-SES and high-SES schools. Teachers in low-SES schools have a greater possibility of being assigned to teach a subject outside their expertise and interest, and this significantly affects their motivation and commitment. This difference does not exist in Australia and Japan, where qualified teachers with subject expertise are equally distributed. Although Australian school administrators face a similar level of pressure to fill teaching vacancies by assigning other teachers to teach the subjects that have a teacher shortage, the pressure does not vary by the level of school SES. To improve teachers' working conditions and students' opportunity to be taught by teachers who are knowledgeable in the subject they are teaching, it is essential that U.S. states provide support to school districts to balance the distribution of qualified teachers and reduce out-of-field teaching.

The noninstructional workload of U.S. teachers both at school and outside school is less than that of Australian and Japanese teachers, and the same as the average of 12 other countries. The level of stress and burn-out reported by Japanese teachers, as well as an increase in the number of teachers taking a leave for mental health reasons, show that the Japanese Government needs to reform teachers' work schedules to reduce noninstructional responsibilities. A national survey showed that Japanese teachers are working 11.3 hours a day on average, and this heavy workload has to be reduced as soon as possible (MEXT, 2007c). The U.S. system of specialized work roles for teaching, counseling, and administrative tasks, with multiple specialists (e.g., school counselors, school psychologists, school safety officers) prevents the overloading of teachers with multiple responsibilities. Yet they are spending close to 3 hours a day outside school on unpaid work, which needs to be minimized or a sufficient allowance needs to be provided.

A comparison of compensation and benefits showed that U.S. teachers are not paid as well as Australian and Japanese teachers, and benefits in the form of allowances and leave are limited compared with those in Australia and Japan. One benefit of U.S. teachers is a shorter contract period that leaves them more vacation time. In reality, many teachers take on summer school teaching responsibilities and other paid work in order to compensate for the low regular salary. The high attrition rates and difficulty attracting qualified candidates into teaching also show that the shorter period of a teaching contract is not a strong incentive for teachers.

A lower rate of salary increase over time is a major barrier to attracting qualified candidates into the teaching profession. Teacher salary is also an important predictor of teacher mobility and retention (Clotfelter et al., 2006; Hanushek et al., 2004). Even the most committed teachers would consider an alternative position with better pay when their salary increase does not match inflation and their salary does not allow an expected living standard for a college graduate. Increasing teachers' salary at least to the average of other comparable professions is a minimum requirement if we want to improve the overall quality of the teaching workforce by attracting more qualified individuals into teaching.

Teacher allowances can be an important financial supplement to the basic salary. Especially the type of allowance that rewards extra work and responsibilities conveys appreciation for teachers' work beyond their regular responsibilities. When teachers are not financially compensated for the extra work and efforts they put in, we cannot expect their commitment or positive work performance. In addition, allowances for supporting professional development, including tuition reimbursement, materials, and travel expenses, can be strong incentives for teachers to engage in continuous professional learning and advancement.

A major obstacle to improving teachers' working conditions through generous allowances in the United States is the differences between districts' financial capacity to offer allowances. Because allowances are not standardized across districts, they cannot be presented as major incentives to attract qualified candidates into the teaching profession. There are some wealthy districts that can offer more generous allowances than those in Australia or Japan, while there are other high-poverty districts that cannot afford even basic teaching materials such as updated textbooks.

The same problem applies to leave. Some districts cannot afford to grant basic maternity leave, whereas some wealthy districts offer an attractive package with extended family leave and study leave, among others.

Extended family leave for child birth or adoption and rearing has a major impact on teachers' personal life and sense of security. When such leave is guaranteed as a right of teachers, it prevents teacher attrition and leads to improvement of the professional status of teaching. The same goes for sabbatical or study leave. Granting these types of leave sends a strong message to teachers that professional development and advancement are highly valued in the teaching profession. These conditions, along with decent teacher salary, have a strong impact on the social status of the teaching profession—but only if salary and benefits are provided equally to all teachers, as in Australia and Japan.

The variation in working conditions across districts in the United States is the major obstacle to improving the working conditions of teachers and the social status of the teaching profession. Without improving the social status of the teaching profession, it is difficult to attract qualified candidates into teaching and improve the overall quality of the teaching workforce. The quality of the teaching profession currently is determined by the free-market principle under which individuals compete for better working conditions in wealthy districts. The result is the huge inequality in teacher quality across districts, which indeed means inequality in students' opportunity to learn.

The principle of merit pay—a highly debated topic in teacher reform, yet a practice that is becoming more popular across the country—is based on the same logic of using the free-market principle and teacher accountability to improve teacher quality. The major problem is that teachers are not competing on the same ground, as their performance depends on their working conditions and the professional support they receive. Competition creates winners and losers, and a resulting inequality in students' learning opportunities. It does not improve the overall quality of the teaching workforce or the social status of the teaching profession. Teacher accountability is a global trend that impacts many countries, and merit pay is a topic of major debate in the United States, Australia, and Japan. Teacher accountability policy does not improve the quality of the teacher workforce as long as there are major disparities in the basic working conditions of teachers, including salary, workload, and work assignment.

RECOMMENDATIONS

Based on the comparisons of teacher workload and assignment, and the examination of teacher salary, allowances, and leave in the United States, Australia, and Japan, we provide the following recommendations regarding the working conditions of U.S. teachers.

1. Focus on improving teacher quality by reforming the working conditions of the entire teacher workforce.

Teaching is a complex and demanding profession that requires professional judgments and decisions based on the immediate situation teachers face on a daily basis. Providing working conditions that support their responsibilities and enhance their motivation and commitment to teaching is critical to improving the quality of the overall teacher workforce. Holding teachers accountable when they are not working under the minimum working conditions for any profession not only will demoralize and discourage teachers, but will lower the social status of the teaching profession. Inequality in working conditions between high-SES and low-SES schools in the United States is a major obstacle to improving the social status of the teaching profession and attracting qualified individuals into teaching. No such inequality in working conditions exists among Australian and Japanese teachers, as their salary, allowances, and leave are standardized at the state, prefecture, or national level.

We also can learn from the problems in Australia and Japan involving workload and assignment. Multiple-subject teaching, prevalent in Australia, and heavy noninstructional duties among Japanese teachers, are what U.S. policymakers and administrators need to avoid. Generous allowances and leave provisions in these countries, as well as equal working conditions, are what they need to work on for improving the social status of the U.S. teaching profession and the overall quality of the teacher workforce.

2. Reduce teaching loads and integrate lesson-planning hours into the regular work schedule.

U.S. teachers are assigned heavy teaching loads compared with teachers in Australia, Japan, and 12 other high-achieving countries, yet they spend the least time on lesson planning. To encourage teachers to spend more time on lesson planning so as to deliver refined, high-quality instruction, it is important to reduce teaching loads and allocate the released time to lesson-planning hours during the regular schedule. When lesson planning is done outside the regular schedule, teachers cannot afford to spend sufficient time on it due to family or other responsibilities. When they are allowed a small amount of time for lesson planning and are assigned to teach so many classes, it is natural that the lessons will focus on procedural skills using worksheets and on homework, which require less preparation time than lessons focused on problem solving and higher order thinking.

Scheduling lesson-planning time during the regular schedule also enhances teachers' opportunity for dialogue and collaboration with other teachers. Isolation is a common problem among U.S. teachers and can lead to a sense of alienation and, in the worst case, resignation. Isolation may be an unavoidable aspect of the professional autonomy granted to U.S. teachers. However, all teachers, especially those new to the profession, need continuous support from their colleagues, school administrators, and students' families and community members. Teaching is a complex and challenging profession, and professional support through teacher collaboration is critical for teachers to successfully fulfill multiple responsibilities.

3. Reduce out-of-field teaching through state support.

Out-of-field teaching is most prevalent in the United States. One out of three teachers teaching mathematics does not have a major in mathematics or mathematics education. Subject major of teachers is a strong predictor of student achievement (Akiba et al., 2007; Goldhaber & Brewer, 1997, 2000; Rowan et al., 1997), and it is critical to reduce out-of-field teaching so as to improve the quality of instruction delivered to students. Teacher shortage is the root of the problem, and a systemic approach to recruitment activities targeted to subject areas of teacher shortage and to hard-to-staff schools, providing strong incentives, is needed, as discussed in Chapter 3. Most low-SES districts, where the shortage is most severe, cannot engage in active recruitment due to fiscal limitations and multiple other problems such as late vacancy notification requirements and teacher union transfer agreements (Levin & Quinn, 2003). Thus, state departments of education need to take the leadership in increasing the number of qualified candidates and promoting equal distribution of qualified teachers among districts, using strong incentives. When the gap in the percentage of high-quality teachers between low-SES and high-SES districts is narrowed, the gap in out-of-field teaching will be minimized as well.

Out-of-field teaching is a critical working condition that discourages even the most committed teachers, yet teachers often are assigned to teach subjects outside their expertise (Ingersoll, 2003b). Many secondary school teachers enter into teaching because they like a subject area and want to share the joy of learning the subject with students. Yet, there is a high possibility that they will be assigned to teach another subject that they have not learned at college or university. They do not feel prepared, and are not motivated, to teach a subject in which they lack content knowledge. Assignment of out-of-field teaching is disrespectful to the subject expertise of teachers, and it demoralizes teachers, leading to higher rates of career change and attrition. This is a practice that hinders the effort to increase the social status of the teaching profession and to attract qualified individuals into teaching. Out-of-field teaching needs to be reduced through state leadership in subject-targeted recruitment efforts.

4. Improve and equalize teacher salaries.

U.S. teachers are not paid as well as Australian and Japanese teachers. Their starting salary is comparable to that of their counterparts, yet a major gap emerges after 15 years of service in the profession. The salary increase for U.S. teachers is less than the cost of living increase, and they are having a difficult time keeping the living standard expected of a college graduate. The percentage of teachers who leave teaching has increased from 5.6% in 1988–89 to 8.4% in 2004–05, and it is expected to continue to increase (Marvel et al., 2006). Teachers in subject areas of shortage, such as mathematics and science, reported "salary or benefits" as an important reason for leaving—the second most common reason after "retirement" (Hampden-Thompson et al., 2008).

Improvement in teacher salaries is essential, given this trend of increasing attrition rates of teachers. The United States invests a smaller portion of total funding in teacher salaries than Australia and Japan, as we saw in the ratio of teacher salary to GDP per capita. While U.S. teachers' average salary is about the same as GDP per capita, Australian teachers are paid 1.3 times and Japanese teachers are paid 1.56 times GDP per capita. It is an issue of how much money a country invests in teacher salaries, and this is a reflection of how important the public thinks teachers are for educating their children.

A challenge in improving teacher salaries is the major disparity in current salaries across the country. The average teacher salary in 2004–05 ranged from $34,039 in South Dakota to $57,760 in Connecticut (American Federation of Teachers, 2007). The disparity at the district level is even larger (Kozol, 1992, 2005). This disparity results from the fact that 44% of public school funding comes from local districts, and districts collect funds through property tax. The different housing prices across regions result in different levels of school funding. As teacher salary is the main expense in school funding, disparity of teacher salary naturally occurs as a result of disparity in school funds across school districts.

Teacher salaries need to be equalized after taking into consideration the differences in the cost of living across regions. Teacher salaries should not differ beyond the difference in the regional cost of living. This is a must for stopping the increasing rates of teacher attrition and attracting qualified individuals into teaching. More investment in education can be achieved with public support, and teachers' social status can be improved, as policymakers in Japan did at the time of teacher shortages in the 1960s.

   5. Improve allowance and leave systems.

   Allowances and leave provided to teachers are other important working conditions that can improve teacher retention and successful recruitment of qualified individuals into teaching. Allowances for extra duties and responsibilities convey appreciation for teachers' extra work, and allowances for professional development purposes such as tuition reimbursement, teaching materials, and travel expenses, are positive incentives for promoting continuous professional learning.

   Family leave for a birth or adoption of a child and child rearing is an important benefit that affects teacher retention. During the 2003–04 academic year, 75% of all public school teachers were female (Strizek, Pittsonberger, Riordan, Lyter, & Orlofsky, 2006). Twelve weeks of unpaid family leave is not sufficient for them, and many of them leave the teaching profession to raise children, contributing to high teacher attrition rates. If extended family leave is offered to teachers with partial salary payment, as in Australia and Japan, fewer teachers would leave the teaching profession.

   Sabbatical leave or study leave are also strong incentives for teachers to remain in teaching and for qualified individuals to enter into teaching. Paid sabbatical leave given to teachers who have served a certain number of years (e.g., 10 years) would increase teacher retention rates and be perceived as a valuable benefit of the teaching profession. Study leave also encourages teachers to engage in professional development and advancement. A deferred salary scheme available to Australian teachers gives greater time flexibility without additional financial cost for employers. Scholarships and paid leave can be made available to teachers on a competitive basis to increase the incentive for professional learning.

   A combination of allowances and leave that recognizes extra work and long years of service is a powerful mechanism to increase teacher retention and facilitate successful recruitment of qualified individuals into teaching. Again, the major variation in allowance and leave packages across U.S. districts makes it difficult to improve the social status of the teaching profession nationwide and the overall quality of the teacher workforce. State departments of education need to work with teacher unions to develop more attractive allowance and leave provisions that are available to all teachers wherever they work.

These recommendations are based on the concept that teachers need to be provided with attractive working conditions for successfully performing teaching responsibilities. Improvement of working conditions is a critical part of a support system for teachers. Another dimension of the support system is professional learning opportunities provided to teachers, which will be discussed in the next chapter.

• C H A P T E R   5 •

Teacher Induction and Professional Development

PROVIDING CONTINUOUS professional learning opportunities is a critical element of a support system for the teaching profession. Teachers need to be equipped with knowledge and techniques of the most updated instructional methods and approaches that have proven effective for improving the learning of their students. As teachers are working with an increasingly diverse student population in terms of race/ethnicity, socioeconomic status, language, and disability, among other factors, they also need to develop their competence to effectively teach their students by connecting teaching content with students' diverse experiences and prior knowledge.

It is critical that beginning teachers be fully supported during the early stages of adjustment and learning through strong induction and mentoring programs. They need to understand the school contexts, including policy, organizational norms, and culture; develop their own instructional approaches and schemes based on their students' knowledge and experiences; and manage the hectic daily schedule and multiple responsibilities of the teaching profession. Induction and mentoring programs are critical for a successful transition from a teacher education program to a school, and they significantly influence the rates of teacher attrition during the early years (Kardos, 2004; Smith & Ingersoll, 2004).

In this chapter, we review and compare the nature of teacher policies and practices concerning induction and professional development in the United States, Australia, and Japan based on policy documents and national statistics available from each country. Drawing on the teacher survey report in the TIMSS 2003 data set, we also compare the frequency of four types of teacher collaboration: (1) discussions about how to teach a particular concept, (2) preparation of instructional materials, (3) visits to another teacher's classroom to observe teaching, and (4) informal observation of one's own lessons by another teacher.

APPROACHES TO PROFESSIONAL LEARNING IN
THE UNITED STATES, AUSTRALIA, AND JAPAN

Title II of the No Child Left Behind Act of 2001 required all teachers to be highly qualified based on the criteria of full certification, possession of a bachelor's degree, and subject-matter competence. To support the professional learning of all teachers, NCLB also required Title I districts to spend at least 5% of their Title I, Part A, funds on professional development. In addition, Title I schools identified for "school improvement" are required to spend 10% of their Title I, Part A, funds for professional development. State departments of education also are required to report the percentage of teachers who participate in high-quality professional development. However, the ambiguity and different definitions across states about what constitutes "high-quality professional development" have resulted in a discrepancy between state reports and teacher survey results concerning what professional development they received (Birman et al., 2007).

Simply requiring the use of funds and reporting of professional development activities does not ensure that all teachers are receiving effective professional development opportunities that help them improve teacher performance and student learning. Many studies have reported the characteristics of successful professional development of teachers (Borasi & Fonzi, 2002; Clarke, 1994; Elmore, 2002; Hawley & Valli, 1999; Loucks-Horsley, Hewson, Love, & Stiles, 1998; Wilson & Berne, 1999). These studies agree that teacher learning is enhanced when teachers are involved in professional development activities with the following characteristics:

1. Sustained and continuous
2. Coherent with teachers' learning goals as well as school missions and reform goals
3. Focused on teaching practices and student learning in the context of actual classrooms
4. Providing opportunities for teacher collaboration

To provide high-quality professional development opportunities with these characteristics to all teachers, it is important that the offerings be well planned and organized along the professional continuum, starting from beginning teacher induction, to mid-career professional development, to teacher leadership development. Such systemic planning and implementation require collaboration and coordination among key stakeholders—state departments of education, teacher education institutions, school districts, school administrators, and teachers. When professional development

activities are organized coherently based on the developmental and regional needs of teachers as well as a shared vision of characteristics of high-
quality teachers, learning opportunities of teachers become meaningful
to them and lead to the improvement of instructional quality and student
learning.

In the United States, professional development activities are offered
by many independent groups, including state professional development
centers, teacher education programs and university instructors, regional
education labs operated by the U.S. Department of Education, private
professional development providers, school districts, and schools, and there
is no systemic effort to coordinate the activities available to teachers. In a
national study of school districts, the Schools and Staffing Survey (SASS),
33% of districts reported that district staff has the primary responsibility
for *deciding professional development content*, while 36% reported that principals have the primary responsibility and 29% that teachers have the
primary responsibility (Choy, Chen, & Bugarin, 2006). The primary responsibility for *designing and planning the activities* was reported to be held
by districts (35%), principals (37%), and teachers (24%). These statistics
show that there is significant variation across districts in who decides professional development content and designs and plans the activities. As a
result, the nature, length, and quality of professional learning opportunities differ greatly across school districts and schools.

This fragmented nature of professional learning activities poses a challenge for offering high-quality professional development consistently to
all teachers. Australia faces a similar challenge. Deciding professional
development content and designing and planning the activities are the responsibilities of regional offices, school districts, or principals, and major
variation in the nature and quality of professional development exists
across districts and schools (Skilbeck & Connell, 2004). This lack of consistency in quality across the country has been considered a major obstacle
to improving the quality of the teacher workforce, and the Australian
Government Quality Teacher Programme was developed to improve professional development opportunities. Since 1999, the AGQTP has supported
school-based sustained action research projects and organized the sharing of resulting teaching and learning resources and best practices. It also
seeks national consistency around the models of good practice through a
comprehensive mapping of current teacher professional learning activities across Australia.

In addition, state and territory teacher registration authorities require
a certain number of hours of professional development to maintain teacher
accreditation. For example, the New South Wales Institute of Teachers
(n.d.a) requires all beginning teachers to achieve the "professional com-

petence" stage within 3 years based on the NSW Professional Teaching Standards. They need to compile evidence of their progress toward "professional competence," including lesson plans, reports on professional learning activities, and notes on teaching observation. An accreditation report is prepared by their supervisors as their application for accreditation (New South Wales Institute of Teachers, 2006). Once they are accredited for "professional competence," they need to complete 100 hours of professional development activities, 50 hours in Institute-registered professional development courses or programs designated as "high-quality" professional development and 50 hours of other formal or informal activities, every 5 years to maintain their accreditation (New South Wales Institute of Teachers, n.d.b). The Victorian Institute of Teaching (n.d.) has the same requirement, completion of 100 hours of professional development aligned with the standards every 5 years for renewal of teacher registration. Thus, these registration requirements, which are supported by but independent of governments, regulate the minimum quantity and quality of professional learning activities for teachers.

In Japan, professional learning opportunities of teachers are highly structured, and activities at the school, district, prefecture, and national levels are well coordinated based on a national model, the teacher professional development implementation system, developed by the Ministry of Education.

Figure 5.1 summarizes these professional development opportunities along the dimensions of the providers (national, prefectural, or local), developmental stages of teaching career (ranging from 1 year to 30 years of service), and types of professional development activities. All of the activities are organized by government agencies (Ministry of Education, prefecture board of education, local board of education) except for on-site and individual professional development, which is designed and implemented by teachers. Professional development activities offered by government agencies often are led by university professors and teacher leaders.

The Ministry of Education emphasizes the importance of considering teacher quality and required competence along the professional life stages (MEXT, 1999). The Ministry identifies three professional life stages: (1) beginning teachers, (2) mid-career teachers, and (3) school administrators. Because school administrator positions are part of the teacher career ladder and experienced teachers become school administrators in Japan, school administrators are part of teachers' professional life stages, although these positions are limited to a small number of teachers.

The Ministry of Education explains that beginning teachers need to develop the quality and competence for instruction, student guidance, and classroom management based on the foundational and theoretical

Figure 5.1. Teacher professional development implementation system mapped on years of teaching experience.

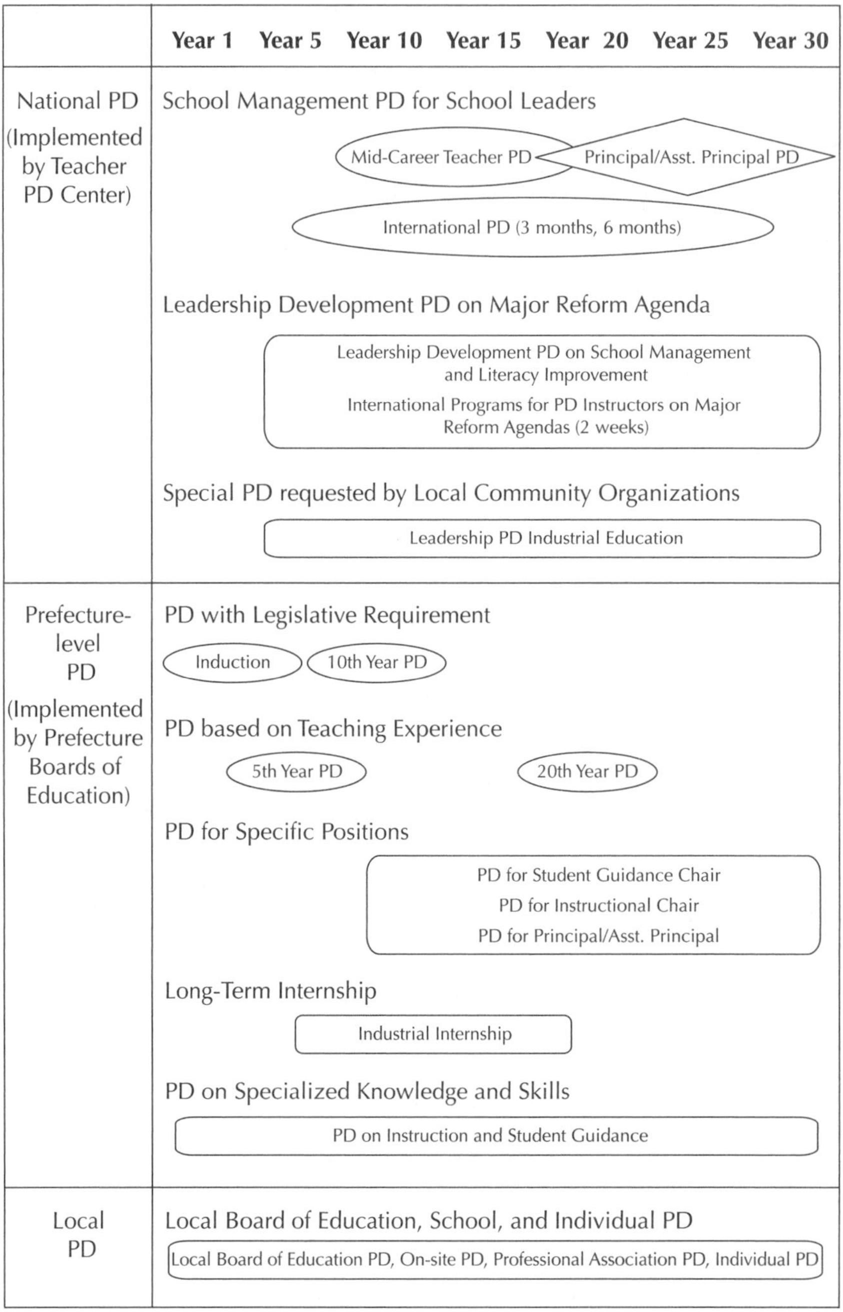

	Year 1 Year 5 Year 10 Year 15 Year 20 Year 25 Year 30
National PD (Implemented by Teacher PD Center)	School Management PD for School Leaders Mid-Career Teacher PD / Principal/Asst. Principal PD International PD (3 months, 6 months) Leadership Development PD on Major Reform Agenda Leadership Development PD on School Management and Literacy Improvement International Programs for PD Instructors on Major Reform Agendas (2 weeks) Special PD requested by Local Community Organizations Leadership PD Industrial Education
Prefecture-level PD (Implemented by Prefecture Boards of Education)	PD with Legislative Requirement Induction 10th Year PD PD based on Teaching Experience 5th Year PD 20th Year PD PD for Specific Positions PD for Student Guidance Chair PD for Instructional Chair PD for Principal/Asst. Principal Long-Term Internship Industrial Internship PD on Specialized Knowledge and Skills PD on Instruction and Student Guidance
Local PD	Local Board of Education, School, and Individual PD Local Board of Education PD, On-site PD, Professional Association PD, Individual PD

knowledge gained in teacher education programs. Mid-career teachers need to develop broader perspectives and deeper knowledge based on extensive experiences in instruction, student guidance, and classroom management. They are expected to take leadership in assisting beginning teachers and participate in school management, which requires quality and competence for leadership and management. School administrators need quality and competence for developing school goals based on a deep understanding of the community and students' characteristics, and for taking leadership in motivating teachers, facilitating collaboration with other educational organizations, and engaging in systemic and dynamic school management. Thus, the professional development opportunities are organized based on these three stages of the professional continuum.

Professional development at the national level offered by the Teacher Professional Development Center operated by the Ministry of Education is mainly for mid-career teachers and school administrators with at least 5 years of teaching experience. Each prefecture board of education also has a Teacher Professional Development Center that offers the majority of professional development activities for teachers, teacher leaders, and school administrators. Induction program for first-year teachers and 10th-year professional development are the two most extensive professional learning opportunities, with legislative requirements for participation. Prefecture boards of education also offer, through the Teacher Professional Development Centers, mandatory 5th-year and 20th-year professional development. Other professional development activities include an internship in industry and specialized professional development offered in subject areas, student guidance, and classroom management.

Local professional development activities are offered either by a local board of education, professional associations or research groups of teachers, or small groups of teachers at schools. These activities may be formal seminars offered by a local board of education, a large-scale public Lesson Study with teacher participants from across a city or prefecture, or an informal study group or on-site Lesson Study within a single school. Lesson Study—the process of instructional improvement in which teachers jointly plan, observe, and discuss lessons—is practiced by every teacher in Japan, and it plays a major role in professional learning among Japanese teachers (Lewis, 2002b; Lewis & Tsuchida, 1997, 1998; Stigler & Hiebert, 1999). Lesson Study has been imported to the United States, and it is practiced by an increasing number of U.S. teachers as well (Lewis, 2002a; Lewis, Perry, & Hurd, 2004; Lewis, Perry, Hurd, & O'Connell, 2006).

Based on the teacher professional development implementation system, which places various professional development opportunities (both formal and informal) along the professional continuum, providers can develop coherent learning opportunities beginning with new teacher induction to 5th-year professional development, to 10th-year and 20th-year professional development. This model also supports the needs of particular responsibilities and subject areas by offering professional development activities for various job positions (e.g., student guidance chair, instructional chair) and various subject areas and classroom issues (e.g., mathematics, literacy, student guidance, classroom management). Based on this model, teachers can see what learning opportunities are available for each career stage and for their professional development needs. In addition, school administrators know the professional learning experiences of teachers and can provide guidance and support to individual teachers based on teacher needs, school missions, and reform goals.

Thus, this systemic organization of professional development opportunities offered to teachers, teacher leaders, and school administrators addresses the first 2 characteristics of effective professional development identified in the United States: (1) sustained and continuous, and (2) coherent with teachers' learning goals as well as school missions and reform goals. The third and fourth characteristics of professional development—(3) focusing on teaching practices and student learning in the context of actual classrooms, and (4) providing opportunities for teacher collaboration—will be examined further through the comparisons of policy and practices concerning induction and professional development in the United States, Australia, and Japan.

TEACHER INDUCTION AND MENTORING

The importance of induction and mentoring programs for new teachers has been pointed out since the 1980s, with the rising attrition rates among beginning teachers. An increasing number of school districts and states are offering induction and mentoring programs to support the smooth transition from teacher education programs to school settings (Smith, 2007). First-year teachers are often overwhelmed with multiple responsibilities in the complexity of school rules, organizational norms, and family and community expectations. New teachers' struggles, without needed induction or mentoring experiences, have been well documented in both the United States (Grossman & Thompson, 2004; Kauffman, Johnson, Kardos, Liu, & Peske, 2002) and Australia (Manuel, 2003; McCormack, Gore, & Thomas, 2006; McCormack & Thomas, 2003). Induction and mentoring programs have proved to increase teacher commitment and lower teacher attrition in the United States (Kardos, 2004; Smith & Ingersoll, 2004).

Feiman-Nemser (2001) identified six central learning tasks of teacher induction:

1. Gaining local knowledge of students, curriculum, and school context
2. Designing responsive curriculum and instruction
3. Enacting a beginning repertoire of approaches to curriculum, instruction, and assessment in purposeful ways
4. Creating a classroom learning community
5. Developing a professional identity
6. Learning in and from practice

Feiman-Nemser pointed out that most induction mandates in the United States do not sufficiently support these learning tasks of new teachers. Previous ethnographies of teacher induction in Japan in comparison with the United States have shown the systemic approach to induction and mentoring programs offered to Japanese teachers and how those programs impact the successful learning of the many tasks identified by Feiman-Nemser (LeTendre, 2000; Shimahara, 2002; Shimahara & Sakai, 1995). What current policy and practices support successful first-year teacher learning in Japan in comparison with the United States and Australia? We will compare teacher induction and mentoring programs in these three countries.

Teacher Policy on Induction and Mentoring

In the United States, determining the content of and delivering induction programs are responsibilities of school districts or schools. State departments of education, however, increasingly have provided funding and required induction and mentoring programs. According to *Education Week*'s "Quality Counts" report (2008), based on a survey of 50 states and the District of Columbia, during the 2007–08 academic year, 22 states (43%) required all new teachers to participate in a state-funded induction program, and 25 states (49%) required their participation in a state-funded mentoring program. Twenty states (39%) also have standards for selecting, training, and/or matching mentors. However, only two states (North Carolina and South Carolina) have a reduced-workload policy for first-year teachers to participate in an induction or mentoring program. School districts also have policies on induction and mentoring, and many teacher education programs offer mentoring to their graduates. Therefore, there is major variation within states in the amount and nature of induction and mentoring programs offered to new teachers.

In Australia, schools select, design, and implement induction or mentoring programs. Despite the strong national leadership for strengthening professional development, beginning teacher induction and mentoring are based on voluntary standards and procedures, and are not mandatory, in most states and territories (Department of Education, Science and Training, 2003). Many states offer mentoring guidelines and toolkits for schools and districts, and some facilitate online professional communities for new teachers. The level of state or territory involvement or leadership in offering mentoring or induction programs varies across the country.

The teacher mentor support program developed by the Victorian Department of Education and Early Childhood Development and delivered by the Victorian Institute of Teaching (2008) has trained 6,491 teachers as mentors, and more than 10,000 new teachers have been supported through the program since 2003. Schools are required to provide a mentor to every new teacher. In Tasmania, the beginning teacher time release program requires schools to give instructional time release of 2 hours a week to beginning teachers for the purpose of participating in a mentoring or induction program or other professional development activities (Tasmania Department of Education, 2007). While mentoring and induction programs are strongly encouraged by state and territory departments of education, the nature of these programs varies because of the lack of requirements and coordination in most states and territories.

In Japan, new teacher induction and mentoring are required by the Education Civil Servant Special Law Title 23 for the purpose of providing practice-based learning opportunities aligned with the daily practices of instruction and classroom management (MEXT, 2007d). New teacher induction consists of on-site induction and off-site induction. All new teachers are required to spend at least 300 hours a year for on-site induction activities, including guidance from off-site and on-site mentors, Lesson Study, and other learning activities. They also are required to spend at least 25 days a year (200 hours a year) for off-site induction activities, including lectures and seminars at the Teacher Development Center, internships in industry, and service learning at a social welfare organization. On-site induction activities address the different needs and concerns of new teachers, while off-site induction activities teach them the knowledge and skills of the best instructional and student guidance practices offered by university professors and veteran teachers, as well as broaden their knowledge and experience through industrial internships or social service learning.

Each first-year teacher is assigned two mentors: one off-site mentor and one on-site mentor. Off-site mentors, who are successful veteran teachers, are required to spend at least 7 hours a week with each new teacher at the new teacher's school. On-site mentors, who are veteran teachers in the same schools as the new teachers, are required to spend at least 3 hours a week with the new teachers on campus. Thus, every new teacher is provided with at least 10 hours of contact a week with veteran teachers to ask questions and seek guidance. Off-site and on-site mentors are released from instructional workload for the hours they spend with new teachers, and school administrators assign part-time teachers to fill the missed instructional hours. Off-site mentors, who usually are assigned four new teachers, are released from instructional responsibilities, as they spend at least 28 hours a week mentoring new teachers at various school locations.

All first-year teachers are provided with a reduction in workload of at least 25 to 30%, which allows them to spend at least 10 hours for on-site induction activities a week and a few days a month for off-site induction activities. This reduced instructional time is filled by part-time teachers. With these intensive mentoring and induction experiences and with significantly reduced workloads provided equally across the country, few Japanese teachers report isolation or a major struggle in the first year of their teaching careers (LeTendre, 2000; Shimahara & Sakai, 1995).

Amounts of Teacher Induction and Mentoring Reported

With the different nature of policy on induction and mentoring across the three countries, what are the levels of implementation in these countries? Based on a nationally representative survey report of U.S. public school teachers in the 2003–04 Schools and Staffing Survey (National Center for Education Statistics, 2008b), 67.1% of teachers reported that they participated in a teacher induction program, and 70.0% worked closely with a master or mentor teacher during the first year of teaching. A similar level of participation was reported in Australia, where 70.5% of early-career teachers reported that they participated in an orientation program designed for new teachers and 70.0% reported that they had a designated mentor (McKenzie, Kos, Walker, & Hong, 2008). These statistics show that while about 70% of teachers participated in induction and mentoring in the United States and Australia, participation is not yet universal, with about 30% of teachers without access to induction or mentoring.

A reduced teaching load needs to be granted to new teachers for participating in induction or mentoring programs. In the United States, only 5.9% of teachers reported that they were given a reduced teaching schedule during the first year (National Center for Education Statistics, 2008b), compared with 46% of Australian teachers who reported that they received a reduced face-to-face teaching workload (McKenzie et al., 2008). These statistics show that while induction and mentoring programs are widely available to teachers in both the United States and Australia, a reduced workload is less common among U.S. teachers than Australian teachers. The amount of time spent on induction or mentoring programs and the nature of these programs are not reported in the United States or Australia.

There are no national statistics on or teacher reports of induction or mentoring programs in Japan. A national survey of prefecture boards of education reported that new teachers spent an average of 10.1 hours for on-site induction each week, and 24.7 days a year for off-site induction during the 2006–07 academic year (MEXT, 2007d). Based on an annual work schedule of 44 weeks and 8 hours scheduled per day, this amounts to a total of 642 hours a year (14.6 hours a week). Interviews with Japanese teachers showed that induction and mentoring programs are universal and considered part of the professional responsibility built into their daily schedule, rather than special opportunities offered by the prefecture or local board of education.

PROFESSIONAL DEVELOPMENT

Continuous professional development opportunities keep teachers knowledgeable about effective practices and offer opportunities for reflection through professional dialogue and discussion with colleagues. When delivered properly, professional development activities promote the practice of student-centered, constructivist instruction (Cohen & Hill, 2000; Desimone, Porter, Garet, Yoon, & Birman, 2002; Garet, Porter, Desimone, Birman, & Yoon, 2001). Based on a survey of 975 teachers in California, Cohen and Hill (2000) found that mathematics teachers who were familiar with leading reform ideas and who participated in professional development on standards-based math curriculum were more likely to practice reform-oriented instruction. Desimone and colleagues (2002) further showed, based on a longitudinal survey of 207 mathematics and science teachers in five states, that standards-based professional development is effective in improving teacher practice of higher order instruction, especially when the activities involve active learning—that is, where teachers are not passive recipients of information and when reform-type activities such as teacher study groups and mentoring were provided (see also Garet et al., 2001).

What policy and practices for professional development currently exist in the United States, Australia, and Japan? State policy documents on professional development in the United States and Australia and a national policy in Japan were reviewed, and national statistics on professional development are compared below.

Teacher Policy on Professional Development

As of the 2007–08 academic year, 41 U.S. states (80%) have formal professional development standards and 24 states (47%) finance professional development for all districts ("Quality Counts," 2008). In addition, 30 states (59%) require districts to align professional development with local priorities and goals. However, a smaller number of states—only 16 (31%)—require districts and schools to set aside time for professional development. These statistics show that while professional development is widely supported by the states, only about half of the states finance professional development, and only one-third of them ensure that teachers are provided with time for professional development activities.

Like induction and mentoring programs, professional development activities are offered by various groups, including professional development centers operated by state departments of education, school districts, schools, and private professional developers. The process of determining the content and implementing the activities varies significantly from district to district, school to school, and even among individual teachers when they are given freedom to choose the professional development content, as in many cases.

In Australia, all states and territories have professional standards for teachers or guidelines for professional learning. All states and territories offer organized and funded professional development activities to meet systemwide priorities such as literacy and citizenship education (Department of Education, Science and Training, 2003). Many states fund action research and/or professional learning teams or groups to promote on-site professional development activities, in addition to those supported through the AGQTP. Some states or territories have a database on all professional development activities offered by the state/territory department of education and regional offices, universities, professional teacher associations, and other training providers; other states or territories offer an online professional learning network for teachers in remote areas. In addition, 61% of schools reported that their teachers participated in national strategic initiatives or other national programs through the AGQTP from 1999 to 2004 (Department of Education, Science and Training, 2005).

In Japan, 10th-year professional development is required by the Education Civil Servant Special Law Title 24 (MEXT, 2007b). For the purpose of further improving teacher quality based on individual competence and characteristics, all teachers who have completed 10 years of service are required to spend 20 days for off-site professional development during summer break, and another 20 days for on-site professional development during the regular academic year. A professional development plan for each teacher is developed by the principal based on the teacher's evaluation results and needs, and the plan is finalized by the local board of education with specific seminars and activities for the teacher.

Off-site professional development activities are offered by the Teacher Professional Development Centers operated by the prefecture boards of education and include case studies, portfolio development, and a research project on a topic of interest within a subject area, student guidance, or classroom management. Teachers also may participate in a short-term internship at a social welfare organization, city hall, library, or industry for service learning purposes. On-site professional development includes Lesson Study and teaching-material research under the guidance of school administrators.

Amount of Professional Development Reported

Based on these policies and legislation in the three countries, what is the level of teacher participation in professional development activities? During the 2003–04 academic year, U.S. teachers reported participating in professional development activities for an average of 66 hours a year, according to a national longitudinal study of NCLB (Birman et al., 2007). Teachers in schools with school improvement status spend longer hours for professional development: 87 hours a year compared with 64 hours in other schools. This is likely the result of NCLB's requirement for schools with improvement status to spend at least 10% of Title I funds for professional development. In Australia, a national survey of teachers showed that teachers in public schools spend an average of 9.5 days, or 76 hours, a year (McKenzie et al., 2008). Australian teachers spend 10 hours more per year for professional development on average than U.S. teachers.

In Japan, a national survey of prefecture boards of education showed that 10th-year teachers spent an average of 18.4 days for on-site professional development and 17.1 days for off-site professional development, a total of 35.5 days, or 284 hours, per year (MEXT, 2007b). Japanese teachers spend about four times as many hours as Australian and U.S. teachers for professional development in their 10th year. The amount of professional development for the other years is less. However, other types of professional development, such as 5th-year and 20th-year professional development and topic-specific professional development activities, are available to teachers throughout the professional continuum. Japanese teachers also engage in Lesson Study informally for the continuous improvement of instructional practices through collaborative lesson planning, lesson observation, and discussion of the effectiveness of particular approaches to enhancing student learning based on student work and student reaction to the approach.

TEACHER COLLABORATION

Opportunities for teacher collaboration are important characteristics of effective professional development programs. Collaboration with colleagues promotes teacher learning of subject content and teaching methods through exchanging feedback on one another's work (Johnson, 1990). It also helps to identify common goals and promote a shared endeavor, which enhances teachers' sense of collegiality and the development of a professional learning community (Little, 1999; McLaughlin & Talbert, 2006). Studies have found that collaboration improves teacher commitment (Kushman, 1992), the practice of constructivist instruction (Desimone et al., 2002; Garet et al., 2001), and student achievement (Goddard, Goddard, & Tschannen-Moran, 2007).

In the 2003 TIMSS, a nationally representative sample of 8th-grade mathematics teachers in the United States, Australia, Japan, and 12 other high-achieving countries were asked, "How often do you have the following types of interactions with other teachers?" with four items:

1. Discussions about how to teach a particular concept
2. Preparation of instructional materials
3. Visits to another teacher's classroom to observe his or her teaching
4. Informal observations of one's lessons by another teacher

Their original responses of "never or almost never," "2 or 3 times per month," "1–3 times per week," and "daily or almost daily" were converted into frequency per month.

Figure 5.2 shows a comparison of frequency of discussions among teachers about how to teach a particular concept. Australian mathematics teachers reported the highest frequency, 6.5 times a month, followed by the teachers in the 12 high-achieving countries, who discuss teaching methods an average of 6.3 times a month. U.S. teachers reported that they discuss teaching methods 5.2 times per month on average. Japanese teachers reported the lowest frequency of collaboration through discussing teaching methods among all the countries, 4.8 times a month.

This result is surprising given the significantly greater amount of time spent for mentoring/induction and professional development among Japanese teachers. It may reflect a cultural difference in what is considered

Figure 5.2. Teacher collaboration: Discussing teaching methods.

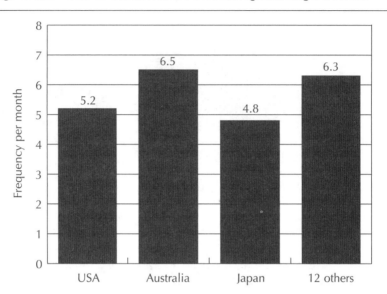

Notes: "12 others" indicates average percentage of Belgium (Flemish), Estonia, Hong Kong, Hungary, Latvia, Malaysia, the Netherlands, the Russian Federation, Singapore, the Slovak Republic, South Korea, and Taiwan. All graphs in this chapter from TIMSS database.

"discussion." If communications about teaching are a daily practice among Japanese teachers, as previous ethnographic studies showed (LeTendre, 2000; Shimahara, 2002; Shimahara & Sakai, 1995), Japanese teachers may not consider a casual communication about teaching methods as discussion. They may consider only formal discussions through teacher team meetings or lesson-planning meetings. In contrast, U.S. and Australian teachers may consider informal communication about teaching methods as discussion if they often work in isolation. In either case, U.S. and Australian teachers experience what they consider discussion of teaching methods more frequently than Japanese teachers.

Figure 5.3 shows the frequency of collaboration in teaching-material preparation. A similar pattern is observed here, with Australian teachers reporting a frequency of 7.0 times a month, followed by 6.0 times a month among U.S. teachers. The frequency among teachers in 12 other countries was 4.7 times a month, and Japanese teachers reported the lowest frequency, only 2.6 times a month. Australian and U.S. teachers are work-

Figure 5.3. Teacher collaboration: Preparing teaching materials.

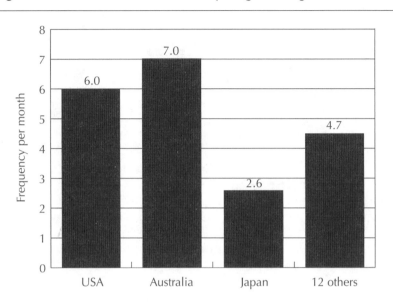

Note: "12 others" indicates average percentage of Belgium (Flemish), Estonia, Hong Kong, Hungary, Latvia, Malaysia, the Netherlands, the Russian Federation, Singapore, the Slovak Republic, South Korea, and Taiwan.

ing together with other teachers at least once or twice each week on preparing teaching materials.

The significantly lower frequency of Japanese teachers' collaboration on preparing teaching materials may be due to the fact that they use textbooks that are closely aligned with the course of study—the national curriculum standards developed by the Ministry of Education. A comparison of textbooks in Japan and the United States has shown major differences in the size of and the number of topics included in the textbooks and teachers' manuals (Lee & Zusho, 2002; Lewis, Tsuchida, & Coleman, 2002; Schmidt, Houang, & Cogan, 2002). Japanese textbooks are thin, yet include all the topics aligned with the course of study, but only those topics. Each student owns the textbooks as well, so there is no need to prepare many additional materials. In the United States, textbooks are teaching resources and materials, from which teachers select appropriate topics and materials. Because U.S. textbooks include so many topics and are not necessarily aligned with state or district content standards, teachers need to spend much time aligning the standards and topics. As a result, they also need to spend a great amount of time developing teaching materials out of available resources, including textbooks. These differences in the nature of textbooks and standards may explain the major difference in the amount of time teachers spend together preparing teaching materials.

The last two types of teacher collaboration—observing lessons and having observers—are more objective measures of collaboration as they allow little room for different interpretations. Figure 5.4 shows the frequency per month of observing a lesson taught by another teacher. Japanese teachers observe another teacher's lesson at least once a month (1.3 times a month on average). Teachers in 12 other countries also observe another teacher's lesson about once a month (1.1 times a month on average). The frequency of lesson observation is lower among U.S. teachers and Australian teachers (mean frequency, 0.7 and 0.5, respectively). The greater frequency of lesson observation among Japanese teachers is likely explained by their practice of Lesson Study, which always involves a lesson observation. Lesson Study also is practiced in other high-achieving East Asian countries such as Hong Kong and Singapore (Ling, Chik, & Pang, 2006; National Institute of Education, 2007), which may contribute to the frequency of lesson observation in the 12 other high-achieving countries.

When we look at Figure 5.5 on the frequency of having observers in one's classroom, however, a different pattern is observed. U.S. teachers

Figure 5.4. Teacher collaboration: Observing lessons.

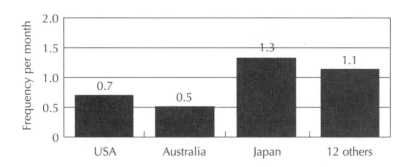

Note: "12 others" indicates average percentage of Belgium (Flemish), Estonia, Hong Kong, Hungary, Latvia, Malaysia, the Netherlands, the Russian Federation, Singapore, the Slovak Republic, South Korea, and Taiwan.

Figure 5.5. Teacher collaboration: Having lessons observed.

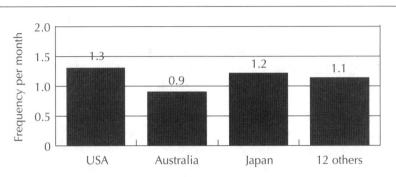

Note: "12 others" indicates average percentage of Belgium (Flemish), Estonia, Hong Kong, Hungary, Latvia, Malaysia, the Netherlands, the Russian Federation, Singapore, the Slovak Republic, South Korea, and Taiwan.

have their lessons observed at least once a month (1.3 times a month on average), as do Japanese teachers (1.2 times on average). Teachers in 12 other countries have their lessons observed 1.1 times a month on average. The mean frequency is less than once a month among Australian teachers. A comparison of Figures 5.4 and 5.5 shows that while the frequency of observing another teacher's lessons and the frequency of having one's lessons observed are about the same for Japanese teachers and teachers in 12 other countries, U.S. and Australian teachers have fewer opportunities to observe lessons than to have their lessons observed.

Lesson Study in Japan usually involves observation of a lesson by multiple teachers (at least 10), who are the team members and observers of Lesson Study. This enhances the frequency of observing lessons among Japanese teachers. However, the common practice of lesson observation by a single teacher or a small number of teachers as part of an informal arrangement (such as having a beginning teacher visit a senior teacher's classroom in the United States) does not create opportunities for many teachers to observe lessons, as Lesson Study does in Japan. In addition, in the United States lesson observation may be done by school administrators as part of teacher evaluation. These informal arrangements for observation by a single teacher or small group of teachers and the use of observation in teacher evaluation increase the overall frequency of having lessons observed, while the opportunity for observing lessons is limited.

SUMMARY

We compared national or state policies on teacher induction, mentoring, and professional development in the United States, Australia, and Japan. We also compared national statistics on the amount and participation rates of mentoring, induction, and professional development offered to teachers as well as teacher reports of collaboration based on the 2003 TIMSS data.

A major difference between Japan and the United States or Australia was found in how teacher learning opportunities are managed. In Japan, teacher induction, mentoring, and professional development are highly structured at the national level and are organized along the teacher professional life stages. The teacher professional development implementation system lists all the teacher learning opportunities available along the professional stages of beginning teachers, mid-career teachers, and school administrators.

Professional development activities are offered at three levels: national, prefecture, and local. Professional development programs at these three levels have different purposes, with national-level activities focusing on leadership and reform agendas; prefecture-level activities focusing on legislatively required professional development (induction and 10th-year professional development) and specialized professional development programs by position (e.g., instructional chair, student guidance chair) and subject areas and professional needs (e.g., mathematics, classroom management); and local activities addressing local needs and teacher-led learning activities. As a whole, this system addresses the needs of all types of teachers at every professional life stage, while ensuring that teacher leaders and school administrators are knowledgeable about educational reforms and competent in leadership skills for meeting national goals.

There are multiple advantages to having a system of structured professional development opportunities offered to teachers along the professional continuum. First, teachers have a clear idea of the content of professional development activities and how various activities are connected and build on one another. They are well informed about what learning opportunities become available as they progress in the professional life stages. This prevents a situation in which teachers do not have access to information about all available professional development or are overwhelmed with too many professional development activities that are not related to one another.

Second, shared learning opportunities promote a better understanding of knowledge and skill among teachers, which enhances a sense of professional community within a school. Because all teachers go through the same professional development along the continuum, such as induction, 5th-year professional development, 10th-year professional development, and 20th-year professional development, they have shared professional knowledge and it becomes easy to develop on-site, teacher-led professional development activities that meet local and teacher needs. School administrators are also aware of the professional development activities each teacher has completed and currently is engaging in, which facilitates effective guidance based on each teacher's needs and promotes effective leadership in developing and improving the instructional capacity of an entire faculty.

Third, the teacher professional development implementation system allows policymakers to take a systemic approach to improving the quality of the teacher workforce. The strong partnerships with teacher education institutions, prefecture boards of education, local boards of education, school administrators, and teachers facilitate a systemic approach to improving professional learning opportunities for school administrators and teachers when new demands for learning or reform directions emerge. The Ministry of Education ensures that all teachers are provided with learning opportunities in the framework of the teacher professional development implementation system through annual surveys of prefecture boards of education. This systemic approach to providing structured and well-articulated professional learning opportunities serves as a strong support system for teachers, as well as workforce management to continuously improve the overall quality of the teacher workforce.

It is important to understand that a systemic approach to providing structured and well-articulated professional learning opportunities to all teachers does not mean that teachers' needs are not addressed or there is no flexibility in professional development content. More than 50% of induction and mentoring and the required 10th-year professional development is devoted to on-site professional development where teachers engage in Lesson Study and other teacher-led activities. Even in off-site professional development, the seminars and activities in the Teacher Professional Development Centers are offered by veteran teachers or university professors. Thus, the national framework allows content flexibility and variation based on teachers' needs and local priorities. The framework ensures that every teacher is provided with professional development opportunities that are connected and coherent along the professional continuum.

The existence of this systemic approach to teachers' learning opportunities results in a greater amount of time devoted to induction (642 hours a year) and 10th-year professional development (284 hours a year) among Japanese teachers compared with Australian and U.S. teachers. Induction and mentoring are widely available to about 70% of U.S. teachers and Australian teachers participating in an induction and mentoring program.

However, the amount of time spent for induction or mentoring programs, as well as types and formats of these programs, are not reported and likely to vary significantly across school districts and schools. For professional development activities, U.S. teachers spend an average of 66 hours a year, and Australian teachers spend 76 hours a year, significantly less than the 284 hours a year spent by Japanese teachers with 10 years of service.

It is important to examine the nature of professional learning opportunities offered to teachers based on the characteristics of effective professional development activities as previously described. According to the NLS–NCLB Teacher Survey (Birman et al., 2007), 54% of secondary mathematics teachers in the United States participated in professional development in mathematics that lasted less than 6 hours, and only 16% of teachers participated in professional development that lasted at least 24 hours during the 2003–04 school year, including the summer of 2004. While more empirical research is needed to identify the length and timespan of professional development that are most effective for improving instruction and student learning, it is clear that 6 hours a year is not sufficient to offer sustained and continuous professional development.

Related to coherence of professional development, a majority of teachers in the NLS–NCLB Teacher Survey reported that their professional development experiences were (1) designed to support state or district standards and/or assessment (66%), and (2) designed as part of a school improvement plan to meet state, district, or school goals (62%) (Birman et al., 2007). However, only 41% reported that the experiences were consistent with their own goals for professional development, and only 18% reported that the experiences were based explicitly on what the teachers had learned in earlier professional development experiences (Birman et al., 2007). These statistics show that a majority of professional development activities are coherent with state, district, or school goals, but fewer activities are addressing teachers' needs and even fewer are connected to one another.

Effective professional development activities also focus on teaching practices and student learning in the context of actual classrooms, but only a small number of activities in the United States have this characteristic. Fewer than 25% of teachers participate in professional development in which they (1) review student work or score assessments (23%), (2) develop and practice using student materials (22%), and (3) conduct a demonstration of a lesson, unit, or skill (16%) (Birman et al., 2007). Lesson Study in Japan has all of these characteristics, and thus all Japanese teachers are exposed to learning activities that focus on teaching practices and student learning in the context of actual classrooms.

The last characteristic of effective professional development activities— opportunities for teacher collaboration—was examined using TIMSS 2003 data on the frequency and types of teacher collaboration among eighth-grade mathematics teachers in the United States, Australia, Japan, and 12 other high-achieving countries. The comparison showed that teacher interaction in discussions about how to teach a particular concept and preparation of teaching materials is most frequent in Australia, followed by 12 other countries, the United States, and Japan. Japanese teachers' frequencies for discussion and teaching-material preparation were the lowest. However, Japanese teachers observe lessons more frequently than any other teachers.

U.S. teachers were about twice more likely to have their lessons observed (1.3 times a month on average) than to observe lessons (0.7 times). The mean frequency of having their lessons observed was 1.2 times a month among Japanese teachers, 1.1 times among teachers in 12 other countries, and 0.9 times among Australian teachers. Among the four types of teacher collaboration, observing lessons taught by other teachers and having lessons observed provide learning opportunities in the context of actual classrooms. By observing teaching approaches and student responses and work, teachers learn what promotes student learning. When their lessons are observed by other teachers, they can receive objective feedback on their instructional approach, teaching materials, and how their approach enhances student learning. These learning opportunities through lesson observation also can promote shared understanding of their instructional goals and effective methods, and a sense of community focused on professional learning. To maximize their professional learning, it is important for U.S. teachers to be provided with more opportunities to observe lessons taught by other teachers.

Finally, to support teachers' professional learning, it is necessary to provide them sufficient time out of their scheduled teaching hours. For new teachers, reduced workload is essential to allow enough time for induction and mentoring programs and to support learning of school and community contexts and development of a repertoire of instructional practices. However, only two states have a reduced-workload policy for first-year teachers, and only 5.9% of U.S. teachers reported that they were given a reduced teaching schedule during the first year. Time for induction and mentoring is embedded in the regular schedule among Japanese teachers, with a 25 to 30% reduction in instructional workload available to all first-year teachers. In Australia, 46% reported that they received a reduced face-to-face teaching workload during the first year.

For teachers at all professional stages in the United States, only 16 states (31%) require districts and schools to set aside time for professional development. Considering the heavy teaching load of 4 hours each day among U.S. teachers, as we showed in Chapter 4, it is difficult for them to engage in sustained and continuous professional development during the regular academic year unless the time is part of their scheduled work hours. Many professional development activities are offered during summer hours outside the teacher contract term. These activities can be offered only on the basis of voluntary participation, and it is not possible to ensure that all teachers receive needed learning opportunities. To provide professional learning opportunities to all teachers as part of the support system for improving the quality of the entire teacher workforce, the time for induction, mentoring, and professional development needs to be embedded in the regular work schedule.

RECOMMENDATIONS

Based on the examination of teacher policies and national statistics on teacher induction, mentoring, and professional development, three recommendations can be offered for U.S. policymakers and state and local educational agencies.

1. Develop a state mapping of professional development activities along the professional continuum.

Each state should map professional development activities along the professional continuum to systematically organize professional learning opportunities available to teachers. All structured professional development programs need to be identified in collaboration with teacher education programs, regional education labs, and professional development centers, and they need to be organized based on their purpose, content, and target groups. Each professional development program needs to be assessed based on state professional development standards and research knowledge on the effective characteristics of professional development activities, and only high-quality programs should be included.

Based on the examination of quality, purpose, content, and target groups of all professional development programs, it is possible to organize high-quality programs for specific learning needs along the professional continuum. Once all high-quality programs are organized in a way coherent with state teacher professional standards, school districts and schools will have clear direction for developing their own professional development plans based on the available programs and their own programs. Each school district and school can integrate on-site, teacher-led professional learning activities into the plan, allowing teachers to add activities that address their needs and those of students and communities in the local context.

When a model or framework for professional development along the professional continuum is developed collaboratively, then all key stakeholders, including teachers, the state department of education, school districts, school administrators, teacher education programs, and professional developers, can work together to support the professional learning of teachers. The learning goals and content are shared, and better communication and understanding among teachers, as well as among all other key stakeholders, are promoted. The state and school district can ensure that learning opportunities are provided to all teachers based on professional stage and needs. This support system for teachers based on a coherent and well-articulated professional development model or framework will improve and sustain the quality of the teaching workforce as a learning profession.

State departments of education also should monitor the implementation of professional development programs based on teacher surveys to ensure that all teachers are receiving high-quality professional development opportunities. The NLS–NCLB Teacher Survey conducted by the U.S. Department of Education reported on the nature of professional learning opportunities offered to teachers based on characteristics of effective professional development such as coherence, opportunities for active learning, and collective participation (Birman et al., 2007). This type of national survey should be disaggregated to the state level to inform the nature of teacher learning opportunities in each state in order to promote the systemic provision of effective professional development activities.

2. Require induction and mentoring of new teachers and a certain amount of professional development, and financially support these programs.

The impact of induction and mentoring programs on the smooth transition into teaching and on teacher retention has been empirically demonstrated, and the importance of these programs for new teachers has been well identified by state departments of education and school districts. Yet, induction and mentoring are not available to all teachers in the United States—about 30% of new teachers have no access to an induction program or a mentor. New teachers are overwhelmed with multiple learning tasks, including gaining local knowledge of students, curriculum, and school context; designing responsive curricula and instruction; and creating a classroom learning community (Feiman-Nemser, 2001), and it is critical that they be provided with strong induction and mentoring programs to support them with effective learning and adjustment into their new professional roles. The provision of mentoring and induction programs to all new teachers is possible only through state requirements and full financial support. The availability and quality of induction and mentoring programs need to be monitored periodically through teacher surveys.

In addition, state departments of education should require a minimum amount of professional development for all teachers. The NLS–NCLB Teacher Survey showed that 23% of mathematics teachers did not participate in any professional development activity in mathematics during 2003–04 (Birman et al., 2007). Without ongoing participation in professional development activities, it is not possible for teachers to improve their instructional practices, as they have no access to updated knowledge and skills and no opportunities to receive feedback and reflect on their instructional practices. The minimum amount needs to be determined based on discussion among all key stakeholders. State financing of the required hours of professional development is necessary to support the continuous professional learning of all teachers. Ensuring that all new teachers receive induction and mentoring programs and all teachers are engaged in continuous professional development activities is a fundamental condition for improving the quality of the teaching workforce.

3. Require a reduced workload for new teachers and embed professional development hours in the regular work schedule.

Time is a critical issue for U.S. teachers, whose instructional workload is heavier than those of teachers in Australia, Japan, and 12 other high-achieving countries. At the same time, U.S. teachers spend less time on lesson planning than teachers in the other countries. When U.S. teachers do not have sufficient time to prepare for their 4 hours of daily lessons, it is unrealistic to expect them to spend time for induction or professional development outside the regular schedule.

New teachers need to be provided with a reduced workload in the first year to support a smooth transition into new job roles and responsibilities. The reduced workload will ensure that new teachers have sufficient time to seek guidance from a mentor and participate in an induction program with other first-year teachers. Also, it will help teachers to engage in learning school and community contexts and developing instructional approaches responsive to their students. They also can observe lessons taught by veteran teachers to learn and discuss instructional methods that are effective for their students.

The time for professional development needs to be embedded in the regular work schedule so that teachers can focus on their learning activities without worrying about their other responsibilities. Accordingly, their instructional workload needs to be reduced to allow sufficient time for professional learning to improve instructional methods. The only way to ensure that all new teachers participate in an induction program and work with a mentor, and that all teachers are guaranteed minimum hours for professional learning, is through state requirements and financial support to cover the required learning activities.

Currently in the United States there is a major variation in professional learning opportunities, ranging from none to more than 24 hours a year. A critical part of the systemic approach to improving the quality of the teacher workforce and improving student learning is a support system to offer coherent and well-articulated learning opportunities to all teachers.

Developing a Coherent Policy
for Improving Teacher Quality

THE UNITED STATES is in the midst of an increasing effort to improve teacher quality. In 1996, the National Commission on Teaching and America's Future produced a report, *What Matters Most: Teaching for America's Future*, and made five recommendations:

1. Get serious about standards, for both students and teachers.
2. Reinvent teacher preparation and professional development.
3. Fix teacher recruitment, and put qualified teachers in every classroom.
4. Encourage and reward teacher knowledge and skills.
5. Create schools that are organized for student and teacher success.

Since then, various federal, state, and local efforts have been made to reform the processes for improving teacher quality. The No Child Left Behind Act of 2001 established "highly qualified teacher" requirements in Title II, the number of alternative teacher certification programs has dramatically increased to address teacher shortages, and more and more states are mandating and supporting teacher induction and professional development.

The focus on improving teacher quality as the major driver of improved student learning and of the country's economy has continued and strengthened, involving every key stakeholder. The National Commission on Teaching and America's Future produced a second report, *No Dream Denied: A Pledge to America's Children* in 2003 to reiterate strategies focusing on improving teacher retention. Then the Teaching Commission, comprising 19 leaders in business, government, and education, produced a report, *Teaching at Risk: A Call to Action*, in 2004 and a follow-up report in 2006. However, this increasing focus on teacher quality is not a phenomenon unique to the United States. It has become a trend for so many countries around the world to reform and implement teacher policy focusing mainly on teacher certification and teacher education (OECD, 2004, 2005; UNESCO Institute for Statistics, 2006).

This book has investigated the major policy and processes to improve teacher quality—(1) teacher recruitment, hiring, and distribution, (2) teachers' working conditions, and (3) teacher induction and professional development—in two high-achieving countries, Australia and Japan, in comparison with the United States. Previous comparative studies have focused on teacher education and teacher certification (Ingersoll, 2007; Schmidt et al., 2007; Wang et al., 2003), and little has been known about the other major processes for improving teacher quality in other countries. The comparisons among the United States, Australia, and Japan in these major processes have revealed that the global trend toward standardization and accountability has impacted teacher policies, yet each country has produced uniquely different policy and processes for improving teacher quality. These unique differences are the source of great lessons we can take from Australia and Japan to improve U.S. teacher policy.

Our in-depth analyses, using both national statistics and document analyses and case studies, have shown that teachers in the three countries work within vastly different policy and school contexts. Yet, the conditions for successful cases in Australia and Japan are strikingly similar to those for successful cases of states and districts reported in U.S. studies, as we will discuss further, below. Several states and districts have dramatically reformed teacher policy around working conditions and professional learning opportunities, yet these cases are the exception to the majority. The fact that Australia and Japan have achieved their success nationwide provides evidence that such success is possible in the United States as well.

We will start this chapter with a summary of findings in previous chapters. Then we will discuss teacher policy coherence in Australia and Japan. Directions for improving U.S. teacher policy will be presented based on the comparative analyses, and specific recommendations will be made on how to improve NCLB. We will conclude with a recommendation for state departments of education to initiate development of a coherent policy for improving teacher quality.

UNITED STATES, AUSTRALIA, AND JAPAN COMPARED

Teacher Qualifications and the Qualification Gap

Teacher qualifications in the three countries were compared along three basic dimensions, using a national sample of mathematics teachers: (1) full certification, (2) mathematics or mathematics education major, and (3) teaching experience of 3 or more years. In the United States, 63.7% of mathematics teachers met all of these qualifications, compared with 68.7%

in Australia, 83.5% in Japan, and 76.4% in eight other high-achieving countries. Not only was the level of U.S. teacher qualifications the lowest among the compared countries, but the gap in teacher qualifications between high-SES schools and low-SES schools in the United States was the largest. While 75.0% of teachers in high-SES schools are considered qualified teachers, only 51.9% of teachers in low-SES schools are qualified. The gap between low-SES and high-SES schools is also observed in Australia, but it is only 8.5% (67.7% vs. 59.2%), significantly smaller than the 23.1% gap (75.0% vs. 51.9%) in the United States. In Japan, an opposite pattern of difference was observed, with 86.3% of mathematics teachers qualified in low-SES schools compared with 78.8% in high-SES schools.

Scholars have pointed to the teacher qualification and knowledge gap in the United States as a serious inequality in student access to qualified teachers (Darling-Hammond, 2006, 2007; Hill, 2007; Ladson-Billings, 2006). Our previous study showed that the U.S. teacher quality gap is the fourth largest among 39 countries around the world (Akiba et al., 2007). Furthermore, the opportunity gap with regard to student access to teachers with a subject major has widened in recent years (Jerald & Ingersoll, 2002). Despite that fact, current major U.S. policies and processes do not address the inequality in student access to qualified teachers.

Teacher Recruitment, Hiring, and Distribution

This book has showed that such inequality is a result of decentralized recruitment and hiring processes and unequal district funding to attract qualified candidates. Both Australia and Japan have established a state-level system to hire and distribute qualified teachers. If we consider that access to a qualified teacher is a right of every child, a state-level systemic approach to ensure equal distribution of qualified teachers is a logical response. While U.S. urban, high-poverty districts respond to teacher shortages by lowering entry standards, Australian state and territory departments of education respond by using strong incentive packages to attract qualified teachers to hard-to-staff remote and rural schools and subject areas of shortage.

We argue that state departments of education are in the best position to ensure students' access to qualified teachers. State departments of education need to take leadership in developing partnerships with school districts, schools, and teacher education programs to establish a systemic approach to recruitment, hiring, and distribution of qualified teachers. Linda Darling-Hammond and Gary Sykes (2003, 2004) argue for the federal government's role in enhancing the supply of qualified teachers targeted to high-needs fields and locations, improving retention of qualified teachers, and creating a national labor market by removing interstate barriers to mobility. While we agree with the importance of federal support and involvement in strengthening the nation's teacher workforce, we believe that states have to play a leadership role because of the localized teacher labor markets, states' closer relationships with teacher education programs and school districts, and their capacity to closely monitor and project teacher supply and demand using state teacher databases.

In Chapter 3 we made four recommendations for state departments of education:

1. Develop a statewide workforce planning and management system through systematizing recruitment, employment, and distribution processes in collaboration with districts and schools.
2. Identify potential teacher candidates other than teacher education graduates, and develop recruitment strategies that consider the characteristics of each target population.
3. Streamline the hiring process at state and district levels, with strong incentives to work in hard-to-staff schools.
4. Monitor the balance of qualified teachers among schools, and use incentives to equalize student access to qualified teachers.

Teachers' Working Conditions

Teachers' working conditions were examined through comparisons of teacher workload and assignment (instructional workload, multiple-subject assignment, out-of-field teaching, and noninstructional workload) and compensation and benefits (salary, allowances, and leave). U.S. teachers have greater formal instructional workloads on average (19.3 hours) than teachers in Australia (17.3 hours), Japan (14.5 hours), and 12 other countries (16.2 hours). However, outside regular school hours, U.S. teachers spend less time on lesson planning (3.8 hours) than teachers in Australia (4.5 hours), Japan (5.1 hours), and 12 other countries (6.4 hours).

Multiple-subject teaching assignments generally were not as prevalent in the United States as in other countries, yet the level of out-of-field teaching was highest in the United States, where 29.7% of mathematics teachers are teaching mathematics without a major in mathematics or mathematics education, compared with 26.4% in Australia, 12.1% in Japan, and 11.1% in 12 other high-achieving countries. The largest gap between high-SES and low-SES schools in the percentage of out-of-field teaching was also observed in the United States. Australian and Japanese teachers, however, spend more hours on noninstructional tasks than U.S. teachers.

In terms of teacher compensation and benefits, U.S. teachers' conditions were not as attractive as those in Australia or Japan. Teacher compensation and benefits are standardized at the state level in Australia and at the national or prefecture level in Japan, in comparison with district-level management of these issues in the United States, which creates major variation and inequality in teacher access to attractive salary and benefits. On a national average, new teacher salaries in the United States are slightly higher than in Australia and Japan, yet a major gap appears after 15 years of service, with Australian and Japanese teachers making about $3,000 and $7,000, respectively, more than U.S. teachers. Australian and Japanese teachers also receive allowances for their extra and overtime work and responsibilities, and housing subsidies. In Australia, teachers in hard-to-staff rural and remote schools receive extra allowances such as bonuses, housing subsidies, and travel to cities. Both Australian and Japanese teachers are given extended parental leave and sabbatical or study leave.

In Chapter 4 we made the following five recommendations:

1. Focus on improving teacher quality by reforming the working conditions of the entire teacher workforce.
2. Reduce teaching loads, and integrate lesson-planning hours into the regular work schedule.
3. Reduce out-of-field teaching through state support.
4. Improve and equalize teacher salaries.
5. Improve allowance and leave systems.

Inequality in working conditions between high-SES and low-SES schools in the United States is a major obstacle to improving the social status of the teaching profession and attracting qualified individuals into teaching. Working conditions should be standardized at the state level by providing greater financial support to high-poverty, inner-city school districts.

Teacher Induction and Professional Development

A comparison of national statistics on teacher induction showed that about 70% of U.S. and Australian teachers participate in induction and mentoring programs, in contrast to 100% in Japan. Only about half of U.S. states require teacher participation in state-funded induction and mentoring programs, and in Australia, beginning teacher induction and mentoring are based on voluntary standards and procedures, not mandatory requirements, in most states and territories. Teacher induction and mentoring are required by national legislation in Japan, and all new teachers are assigned two mentors (on-site and off-site). They spend 14.6 hours a week for induction and mentoring, which are built into their regular weekly schedule. Only 5.9% of U.S. teachers are given a reduced workload in their first year, in comparison with 46% of Australian teachers and 100% of Japanese teachers.

For professional development, U.S. teachers spend an average of 66 hours a year, in comparison with 76 hours in Australia and 284 hours in Japan (10th-year teachers). Japanese professional development programs and activities are organized along teachers' professional life stages based on the national teacher professional development implementation system, and professional learning opportunities are required and fully supported by the Ministry of Education. In the United States, 24 states finance professional development for all districts, but only 16 states (31%) require districts and schools to set aside time for professional development. In Australia, the AGQTP has been offering, through multiple providers, high-quality national and state professional development programs since 1999 to solve the problem of fragmented learning opportunities, and participation in professional development in state-registered programs is required for teacher registration renewal or teacher accreditation.

A comparison of the frequency of teacher collaboration based on mathematics teachers' reporting showed that while U.S. and Australian teachers spend more time discussing how to teach a particular concept and preparing teaching materials than Japanese teachers, they are less likely than Japanese teachers to observe lessons of their colleagues. U.S. teachers were about twice as likely to have their lessons observed as to observe other teachers' lessons (1.3 and 0.7 times a month, respectively). By observing teaching approaches and student responses and work, teachers can learn what works for promoting student learning in their school contexts. The learning opportunities through lesson observation also can promote shared understanding of their instructional goals and effective methods, and a sense of community focused on professional learning. It is important that U.S. teachers be provided with more opportunities to observe lessons taught by other teachers, to maximize their professional learning opportunities.

Based on these comparisons, we made three recommendations in Chapter 5:

1. Develop a state mapping of professional development activities along the professional continuum.
2. Require induction and mentoring of new teachers and a certain amount of professional development, and financially support these programs.

3. Require a reduced workload for new teachers and embed professional development hours in the regular work schedule.

Teacher Education

Teacher education is another important process for improving teacher quality, but was beyond the scope of this book. However, we would like to briefly discuss teacher education because of its importance. Previous comparative studies on teacher education have found that high-achieving countries have more rigorous standards with high-stakes screening at multiple times—entry into a teacher education program, evaluation of field experience, exit from a teacher education program, or certification—whereas in the United States, teacher licensure testing is the only major high-stakes criterion for determining who becomes a teacher (Wang et al., 2003). In addition, in high-achieving countries, the top one third of college students in academic standing are recruited into teaching using selective entry requirements for teacher education programs (McKinsey & Company, 2007).

In Japan and Australia, teacher education programs are undergoing reforms to improve the quality of teaching internships, better integrate theory and practice, and develop partnerships with local schools. The standards for teacher training are becoming more rigorous; the recent establishment of Teacher Professional Graduate Schools in Japan for practicing teachers to advance their training and quality represents this trend. In Japan, all teacher candidates are required to graduate from teacher education programs accredited by the Ministry of Education. In Australia, all teacher education programs, including alternative programs, have to go through a rigorous accreditation process by a state/territory registration authority. National accreditation currently is being developed, which will further raise the quality of standards for teacher education programs. Thus, the common trend for improving the quality of the teacher workforce in these high-achieving countries is through raising standards throughout teacher education programs, including entry, coursework and student teaching, and graduation and certification. Based on these observations and previous studies, it is unlikely that the quality of the U.S. teacher workforce will be improved through deregulating or lowering standards. It is important that both traditional and alternative teacher education programs in the United States, with support from state departments of education, develop and maintain high admission standards in order to ensure selection of the most qualified candidates.

POLICY COHERENCE IN THE UNITED STATES, AUSTRALIA, AND JAPAN

In Chapter 1, we introduced the conceptual model of a coherent policy for improving teacher quality and argued for the importance of a systemic approach to (1) recruiting and training, (2) hiring and distributing, and (3) continuously supporting and retaining teachers. If we are to systematically improve the quality of the U.S. teaching workforce, we need a system that simultaneously addresses multiple processes, based on a vision of the characteristics of high-quality teachers shared among national, state, and local stakeholders.

The importance of a coherent policy is not a new idea. Prominent policy researchers—Susan Fuhrman (1993), Marshall S. Smith and Jennifer O'Day (1991), and David Cohen and Heather C. Hill (2001)—have advocated for the importance of coherence or consistency in policy to achieve systemic school reforms for improving student learning. They pointed out that a coherent policy needs to be developed around rigorous standards with clear definitions of learning goals (Fuhrman, 1993; Smith & O'Day, 1991), and that such a policy is likely to succeed when student assessment, curriculum, and teacher professional learning are closely aligned with the standards (Cohen & Hill, 2001). With the central role teachers play in the success of educational reforms and the complexity and fragmentation of current teacher policies implemented by multiple agencies, we argue for a systemic approach to improving teacher quality through a coherent teacher policy based on teacher professional standards.

Through comparative analyses of key teacher policies and processes concerning (1) recruitment, hiring, and distribution, (2) working conditions, and (3) professional learning opportunities in the United States, Australia, and Japan, we used a holistic method to examine each country's approach to improving the quality of the teacher workforce. We found that Japan and Australia take a systemic approach to improving teacher quality by focusing on professional development. Both countries have a system in place at the state or prefecture level to select and hire the most qualified candidates. State/territory departments of education in Australia engage in active recruitment with strong incentives to attract qualified teachers into hard-to-staff rural and remote schools and in subject areas of teacher shortage. Teacher compensation and benefits are standardized at the state/territory level in Australia and at the national level in Japan, ensuring equal teacher access to attractive salary, allowances, and personal and study leave.

The importance of a systemic approach to improving the quality of the teacher workforce also is expressed in recent national initiatives in

Australia and Japan. In 2007, the Australian Ministerial Council on Education, Employment, Training and Youth Affairs agreed to the development of a strategic framework for a national approach to workforce planning in education, and designated this responsibility to the Improving Teacher and School Leader Capacity Working Group, comprising representatives from each state/territory, the Australian Government, the National Catholic Education Commission, and the Independent Schools Council of Australia (DEEWR, 2008).

In Japan, the Ministry of Education recently developed a framework for a systemic approach to teacher education, hiring, and professional development (MEXT, 2008b). The framework has three major components—teacher education, hiring, and professional development—which are integrated through partnerships among the Ministry of Education, teacher education programs, and prefecture and local boards of education. The importance of human resource management is emphasized by the establishment of a new teacher evaluation system and management of teachers who do not meet the standards.

In contrast, there exists no such national approach to teacher workforce planning and management in the United States. The major processes to improve teacher quality in the United States are decentralized at the district or school level, and unequal funding and capacity to implement these processes have resulted in major inequality across districts and schools in student access to qualified teachers. Although most states have teacher professional standards, a vision of high-quality teachers is not shared among state departments of education, school districts, teacher educators, professional development providers, administrators, teachers, and community members. There is no established mechanism to develop partnerships and collaboration among these key stakeholders, and there is a pattern of federal and state requirements being modified and redefined at implementation levels by school districts, administrators, and teachers.

The Australian Government seems to have established consultation and discussion procedures with key stakeholders that are used whenever a national initiative or reform is developed. The development of a policy is always initiated with a thorough review of national and international research on the topic by university researchers or researchers at the Australian Council for Educational Research. All key stakeholders, including representatives from states and territories, teacher professional associations, principal associations, teacher education institutions, teacher unions, researchers, and teachers, are consulted through conferences, and feedback across the country is gathered and integrated into the development process. Teachers are often part of the task force that develops a national policy or initiative for teachers. For example, for the development of the National

Professional Standards for Advanced Teaching and for Principals, a group of teachers and principals produced a first draft of capabilities for advanced teacher and principal standards (Teaching Australia, 2008). The developmental process and opportunities for input from anyone concerned are well communicated through the publication of consultation papers.

Such a mechanism for partnership and collaboration exists among the Ministry of Education, prefecture and local boards of education, and teacher education programs in Japan, although it usually does not involve teachers. This has resulted in multiple educational reforms that simply overloaded teachers without a clear impact for improvement of teacher practice or student learning. However, teachers are deeply involved in the development and implementation of professional development activities. Teacher leaders are hired as instructors and facilitators of off-site professional development programs, and they actively serve as teacher mentors. The full support of the Ministry of Education for professional development, and protection of teacher time for it, has allowed innovative teaching and instructional methods to be developed through practices of Lesson Study, many of which have been disseminated across the country in books and journals published by teachers.

It is important to understand, however, that neither Japan nor Australia has yet achieved a coherent policy for improving teacher quality. Induction and mentoring programs and professional development programs are still fragmented in Australia, and about 30% of new teachers still have no access to induction or mentoring programs. Japanese teachers' workload needs a major improvement, especially with respect to noninstructional duties. These countries are facing challenges, and these challenges offer insights into the development of a coherent teacher policy in the United States. In addition, our comparative analyses shed light on the strengths in the United States for moving toward the development of a coherent teacher policy. We will discuss the directions for improving U.S. teacher policy based on lessons from this comparative study.

ROAD MAP FOR IMPROVING U.S. TEACHER POLICY

Building on U.S. Strengths

A major benefit of cross-national comparisons is the ability to better understand our own system through the perspective of others. In-depth analyses of major processes to improve teacher quality in the United States, Australia, and Japan led us to identify two strengths unique to the United States. One is the advanced teacher data system, and the other is high-quality national professional standards that integrate a teacher performance assessment system as developed by the NBPTS and INTASC.

The U.S. Department of Education, through the work of the National Center for Education Statistics, has gathered systemic data on the teacher workforce. The Schools and Staffing Survey collects nationally representative, longitudinal data from districts, schools, and teachers to identify teacher attrition, turnover, and conditions and factors that lead to them. It also collects extensive data on teacher professional learning opportunities (induction and professional development), teachers' working conditions, and teacher background information, perceptions, and attitudes toward teaching. The implementation of 2-year data collection (main and follow-up surveys) every 5 years allows the identification of trends in the characteristics of the teacher labor market and teacher workforce over time. SASS data were considered an exemplary model for the development of a national teacher data set recently begun in Australia as part of a national approach to workforce planning in education (DEEWR, 2008). Neither Australia nor Japan currently has such an advanced national data system.

We recommend that the United States build on this infrastructure of teacher data management in developing a coherent policy for improving the teacher workforce. The SASS data should be modified by collecting representative state data to create a national sample, as in the National Assessment of Educational Progress. This would allow each state to analyze and understand teacher labor markets and teacher workforce characteristics and to use the data to develop a systemic statewide approach to teacher recruitment, hiring, and retention in combination with its individual state database. An increasing number of states are developing longitudinal databases that link district, school, teacher, and student data for promoting data-based policy and decision making under the U.S. Department of Education Statewide Longitudinal Data Systems Grant Program, which has funded a total US$115 million to 27 states since 2005. Using both state-disaggregated SASS data and state longitudinal data, state departments of education can be better informed about the direction for developing a coherent policy for improving the teacher workforce.

The second strength is well-established professional standards and teacher assessment system developed by the NBPTS and INTASC. The NBPTS is an independent professional body of teachers that provides advanced certification to teachers who attain its standards for highly accomplished practice. A rigorous assessment process, using portfolio entries and the assessment center, is involved in the decision to grant the NBPTS certification, with a passing rate of about 40%. The INTASC (1992) is a program of the Council of Chief State School Officers, and it developed the

Model Standards for Beginning Teacher Licensing, Assessment and Development for states to use in making initial licensing decisions. The INTASC also developed a model performance assessment in the form of a candidate portfolio in mathematics, English/language arts, and science that is aligned with its standards. These standards and assessment systems have been highly regarded in Australia and considered as models for the development of its national standards (Ingvarson, 2002; Ingvarson & Kleinhenz, 2003). These U.S. standards and assessment systems also served as models for the suggested development of a standards-based career structure for teachers in Australia, which ties advanced certification statuses such as "accomplished teacher" and "leading teacher" to salary increases (Dinham, Ingvarson, & Kleinhenz, 2008).

The NBPTS and INTASC standards will serve as great tools for building consensus for a vision of high-quality teachers among key stakeholders. These standards are well recognized by the teaching profession and state departments of education, and use of the assessment systems for initial licensure and teacher evaluation for salary increases will promote both consistency among standards, licensing, and teacher evaluation and exemplary teaching practice. Despite establishing these standards and assessment systems in the early 1990s, ahead of other, high-achieving countries, the United States is now behind Australia in developing a national teacher workforce planning and management system. Australia's system builds consensus on teacher professional standards across the country and aligns teacher education, recruitment, and hiring processes, and professional learning opportunities with state and national standards. Using the NBPTS and INTASC standards to build consensus among key stakeholders on a vision of high-quality teachers will be an important first step in developing a coherent policy for improving the teacher workforce through systemic approaches to recruitment; training, hiring, and distribution; and provision of professional learning opportunities.

Learning from Challenges in Australia and Japan

Another benefit of cross-national comparison is that it offers an opportunity to learn from challenges faced by other countries in the implementation of educational policy or reform. A major challenge in staffing faced by Australia is the concentration of new teachers in hard-to-staff, high-poverty rural and remote schools. While beginning teachers with fewer than 3 years of teaching experience constitute only 1.5% of teachers in high-SES schools, they account for 17.2% in low-SES schools, according to the TIMSS data. The priority transfer to an urban or suburban school after serving a few years in a rural or remote school, as part of the incentive to work in hard-to-staff schools, created the pattern of new teachers working in these schools to "do their time" until they could move to an urban or suburban location. The harsh working conditions and lack of professional learning opportunities in rural and remote schools contribute to high turnover rates.

What we can learn from this situation is the importance of improving working conditions and learning opportunities of teachers in hard-to-staff schools in order for incentive programs to work effectively. Unless high-poverty urban schools are fully supported by districts and state departments of education in improving working conditions—reducing instructional workloads, abolishing out-of-field teaching, improving teacher materials and resources, and ensuring teachers' safety at school—and offering high-quality induction and continuous professional development that address local needs, new incentive programs to attract high-quality teachers are likely to create the same revolving-door situation as in Australia. It is important that this "support" system be in place before the implementation of incentive programs to attract high-quality teachers to hard-to-staff schools.

A lesson from Japan is the importance of involving teachers in the decision-making and developmental processes for major national policy and reform. Teachers' voices were absent from the development of a major teacher policy—the teacher certification renewal system. As a result, this policy required teachers to participate in 30 additional hours of professional development offered by universities and approved by the Ministry of Education for certification renewal, without addressing the major obstacle faced by Japanese teachers—excessive working hours (11.3 hours a day on average). Thus, this policy is not likely to succeed in further improving the quality of teachers in Japan.

Teacher participation in the development of a national teacher policy, as practiced in Australia, will lead to teacher support of the policy and its successful implementation. When teachers' voices are heard, the pressing needs of teachers become apparent. Unless a national teacher policy addresses teachers' needs, the policy is likely to fail. Unless the policy is aligned with what teachers believe will benefit their students, it will receive no support from teachers. And unless teachers feel they are supported for improving teaching, the ultimate goal of improving student learning will never be achieved. By focusing on partnerships and agreements with teachers and other key stakeholders, rather than directives and mandates, a national teacher policy such as Title II of No Child Left Behind has a greater chance of achieving its goal of improving teacher quality and student learning.

Learning from Successful Cases in the United States

The critics of cross-national comparative policy studies express skepticism that anything useful in the U.S. context can be learned from other countries. Critics may say, "Yeah, those policies and reforms work in Japan and Australia, but we are nothing like these countries," or "We believe in freedom and individual rights here. Federal involvement in education like in other centralized countries only deteriorates our best local practices." Some may even say, "Yes, Japanese students achieve better than we do, but they have higher suicide rates, right?" We have heard these comments over and over when we present or communicate our work. Our research has proved, fortunately, that none of these comments has an empirical basis.

Indeed, in our recommendations for improving teacher quality, we found a major similarity between those drawn from cross-national comparative analyses of teacher policy and those drawn from successful U.S. state and district cases. We will review these well-documented cases here. Two successful state cases are from Connecticut and North Carolina (Darling-Hammond & Sykes, 2003; Wilson et al., 2001). Five successful district cases are from New York City, Community School District #2 (New York City), New Haven (California), San Diego (California), and Philadelphia (for first four cases, see Darling-Hammond & Sykes, 2003; for Philadelphia, see Neild, Useem, Travers, & Lesnick, 2003). In these cases teacher policy focused on (1) raising the standards for teacher education, licensure, and hiring, (2) improving teacher salary, (3) strengthening recruitment and hiring processes, and (4) providing high-quality mentoring and professional development to teachers.

Both North Carolina and Connecticut saw major student achievement gains and narrowed the minority–White achievement gap by raising standards for teacher education and licensure. North Carolina requires all schools of education to be accredited by the National Council for Accreditation of Teacher Education, and it supported the development of professional development schools partnered with schools of education. Connecticut requires a subject major in the area of teaching, more pedagogical training, and competence in teaching reading and students with special needs. All teachers must complete a master's degree and pass a rigorous performance assessment to obtain a professional license. In addition, New Haven hired only fully certified teachers, in contrast to neighboring districts where more than 20% of teachers were not certified, and collaborated with a high-quality alternative certification program. Combined with strong incentives and a reformed hiring process, the district achieved a teacher surplus within a short time frame.

Successful states and districts also increased teacher salary to attract qualified candidates into teaching. Connecticut increased the average teacher salary from $29,437 in 1986 to $47,823 in 1991, and equalized the salaries across the state with state financial aid. North Carolina provides notable salary increases for National Board Certified Teachers. New York City also increased the average teacher salary by 16% and that for beginning teachers by more than 20% to offer competitive salaries with surrounding suburban districts, which resulted in filling all vacancies by July and increased the percentage of fully certified teachers to 90% in 2002.

All of these states and districts also strengthened recruitment and hiring processes. North Carolina created the North Carolina teaching fellows program, which pays all the costs associated with teacher training for academically strong students in return for a few years of teaching. Connecticut also offers service scholarships and forgivable loans to high-quality candidates and provides financial incentives to teach in hard-to-staff schools. New Haven, San Diego, and Philadelphia streamlined the hiring process by developing an online application and tracking system and making early offers to highly qualified candidates. They also created multiple financial incentives, including bonuses for teaching in high-needs schools and subjects and tuition reimbursement, and reached out to teachers in other states and overseas.

Providing high-quality induction and professional development was considered the critical factor for supporting professional learning and improving teacher retention. Connecticut and Philadelphia provided trained mentors/coaches to all new teachers, and New Haven implemented a beginning teacher support and assessment program that assigned trained mentors to teachers in their first 2 years and gave released time to the mentors. North Carolina created the North Carolina Center for the Advancement of Teaching (professional development academies), and Connecticut and New York City's Community School District 2 require teachers to engage in continuous professional development.

These policies and processes to improve teacher quality are aligned with our recommendations, and show that these changes are possible in the U.S. context. The difference between the United States and Australia or Japan is that these successful cases are limited to a small number of U.S. states and districts, while in Australia and Japan the policies have been implemented across the countries. Thus, the recommendations we made in Chapters 3–5 relate to how to scale up these efforts across the nation with strong leadership from state departments of education and with federal support. One major way for the federal government to support the development of a coherent policy at the state level is to improve the No Child Left Behind Act.

HOW SHOULD NCLB BE IMPROVED?

We discussed the problems of Title II of No Child Left Behind in Chapter 2. While national policies in Australia and Japan focus on professional development, Title II of NCLB focuses on the requirements for entry-level qualification. Because this policy did not address the root problems of unequal district funding and the resulting inequality in teacher salary and working conditions, the "highly qualified" teacher requirements were redefined by the states, creating major variation in entry standards. We argue that three elements of NCLB need to be changed:

1. Stop labeling districts and schools by publicly announcing those "needing improvement."
2. Specify the use of Title II funds for developing teacher workforce planning and management systems aligned with teacher professional standards.
3. Focus on teacher support systems rather than teacher accountability systems.

First, public announcement of schools not meeting adequate yearly progress significantly hinders districts' efforts to attract qualified teachers for the students who need them the most. Using such a form of accountability when there is a major inequality in district funding and capacity to hire qualified teachers only widens the opportunity gap for students to be taught by qualified teachers along the lines of socioeconomic status. If the purpose of No Child Left Behind is to improve student learning by assigning highly qualified teachers to all students, it should be clear that labeling districts and schools as failing not only drives highly qualified teachers away from these districts and schools, but also denies students' right to be taught by highly qualified teachers. Students' choice to transfer to another school, as specified in Title I of NCLB, is a privilege practiced by only a small group of well-informed parents who know how the system works, and this does not ensure students' right to access highly qualified teachers.

Second, Title II funds distributed to states need to be used for developing a coherent policy for teacher workforce planning and management based on teacher professional standards. State departments of education need to develop a strategic plan to systematically approach the major processes for improving teacher quality—recruitment and training, hiring and distribution, and continuous support through improving working conditions and professional learning opportunities of teachers. The U.S. Department of Education should take the leadership in developing a strong partnership between the federal and state departments to build consensus on the directions for improving teacher quality and student learning based on discussions of the current state of quality of the U.S. teacher workforce as well as the unequal distribution of qualified teachers.

Once national consensus on the general direction has been achieved, each state can develop its own approach to systematically reform major processes for improving teacher quality, with federal financial support. State models for teacher workforce planning and management should be shared among states, and each state's progress based on state and national data should be reported annually. Without such a partnership between the federal and state departments to promote consensus building, and continuous federal funding support to achieve the shared goal, successful teacher policy implementations that improve teacher practice and student learning will continue to be limited to a small number of states and districts.

Finally, NCLB needs to focus on a teacher support system rather than a teacher accountability system. The U.S. Department of Education approved the provision of US$98 million in 2008 and US$200 million in 2009 under the Teacher Incentive Fund to districts, states, and nonprofit organizations to: (1) develop and implement innovative compensation systems to attract the best candidates into teaching and leadership, (2) provide financial incentives for teachers and principals who raise student achievement, and (3) close the achievement gap in the highest needs schools (U.S. Department of Education, 2008b). In a key policy letter to the Chief State School Officers, Margaret Spellings supported "value-added" methods to determine a teacher compensation system that links teachers with their students' achievement gains, statistically controlling for students' background characteristics (U.S. Department of Education, 2008b). The Teacher Incentive Fund represents increasing focus on teacher accountability through financial incentives tied to student achievement.

We argue, based on our comparative analyses, that a teacher compensation system using value-added methods does not support teachers in working toward a vision of high-quality teachers. Student outcomes used in value-added methods are limited to standardized assessment results that do not measure higher order thinking and problem-solving skills. When teachers' salary is determined by such a narrow measure of student learning, classroom teaching becomes oriented toward test-taking skills. In addition, individual merit pay based on student scores does not promote collaboration among teachers, or teacher leadership to support new teachers. Most important, there is no successful case of teacher compensation systems using value-added methods in other countries or in U.S. states or districts, although many districts have experimented with such methods.

Previous successful cases abroad and in the United States point to the greater promise of improvement of teacher salary across the board and use of additional incentives in the form of bonuses, tuition reimbursement, and housing subsidies for working in hard-to-staff schools and in high-needs subject areas. These methods increase the professional status of teachers and attract more-capable candidates into teaching, especially in hard-to-staff schools. A synthesis of empirical studies also showed that NBPTS's career ladder system and knowledge- and skill-based pay system hold greater promise than do value-added methods (Corcoran, 2007). All of these systems support teachers in working toward achieving a vision of high-quality teachers who engage in continuous professional development, collaborate with other teachers, and seek effective methods for teaching students with the greatest needs. These teacher evaluation and compensation systems are coherent with professional standards for teachers and function as part of a support system to promote continuous professional learning.

In summary, we cannot improve teacher practice and student learning without a teacher support system. Both Australia and Japan have established strong support systems to improve teachers' working conditions and professional learning opportunities, instead of focusing on a teacher accountability system. Provisions of NCLB need to be modified to shift its focus from accountability to school and teacher support, and to promote state efforts to develop coherent policies for improving the quality of the U.S. teacher workforce.

DEVELOPING A COHERENT TEACHER POLICY

We conclude the book with a recommendation for state departments of education regarding the steps they could take to develop a coherent teacher policy. The first step is to analyze state data on teachers to understand basic teacher qualifications, distribution of qualified teachers across districts and schools, out-of-field teaching, and characteristics of state teacher labor markets. Most states collect basic data on teacher qualifications, including certification, subject major, teaching experience, and highest degree earned. By analyzing these characteristics at district and school levels, states can examine the distribution of teachers with basic qualifications across the state. In addition, using certification and subject major data, the level of out-of-field teaching can be analyzed. For the characteristics of teacher labor markets, states can compare the number of certified individuals and number of hired teachers and compute turnover and attrition rates by district and school characteristics (poverty level, percentage of ethnic minority students, school location). In addition, by using certification and citizenship data, states can examine the labor market flow from other states or overseas. These data serve as an important reference for identifying problems and issues that need to be dealt with.

Second, each state department of education can form a task force for improving teacher quality through a coherent policy. The task force needs to include representatives from all key stakeholders—teacher education programs, teacher professional associations, teacher unions, school districts, school board associations, professional development providers, school principal associations, education researchers, and most important, teachers. The state department of education can provide state teacher data to show the current conditions of teachers and a framework for the major processes to be modified and enhanced to improve teacher quality—teacher education; recruitment, hiring, and distribution; improving working conditions; and providing high-quality induction and professional development opportunities. The task force can start with problem identification and consensus building on the vision of high-quality teachers, using either state teacher professional standards or other national teacher professional standards.

Third, the task force can develop an action plan for adopting the identified processes to improve teacher quality. A subcommittee or group may be formed for each process (e.g., teacher education or hiring) to address the complexity of the issues. Complete information about federal and state funding should be made available to the task force upfront, so that it can develop a financially feasible plan. This action plan involves the designation of responsibility for each process among key agencies and the reallocation of responsibilities if needed. For example, determining who should be in charge of teacher hiring will require careful discussion as both districts and schools have held this responsibility. Responsibilities need to be delegated based on who would be best positioned to effectively work toward achieving the shared goal of improving teacher quality. Responsibilities may be delegated to one group, or shared by multiple groups through collaboration and coordination. The task force also needs to develop the timeline for achieving the goal and a process to keep track of the progress along the way. Once a draft action plan has been developed, the task force distributes the draft as a consultation paper for gathering feedback across the state, and a state conference, inviting key stakeholders, can be convened to engage in in-depth discussion of the action plan to further refine and finalize it.

This process of consensus building among key stakeholders and their central involvement in the development of an action plan is critical for developing a coherent teacher policy. It probably will take several years to develop an action plan that is agreed upon by all key stakeholders. The commitment and dedication of major stakeholders are required in order to develop a coherent support system for teachers to improve teaching and student learning. The stakeholders also need to believe in students' right to be taught by high-quality teachers regardless of the school's poverty level or location, and to support equal distribution of high-quality teachers across the state. When all key stakeholders agree on this fundamental goal of providing high-quality teachers to every student, they will engage in concerted efforts to implement the action plan for improving the quality of the teacher workforce. Our study proved that developing a coherent teacher policy is not only "what should be done," but also "what can be done" in the United States.

References

AEU Victorian Branch. (2008). *AEU News: The deal is done* (Report Vol. 14, issue 4). Abbotsford, Victoria, Australia: Author.

Akiba, M. (2004). Nature and correlates of *Ijime*—Bullying in Japanese middle school. *International Journal of Educational Research, 41*(3), 216–236.

Akiba, M. (2008). Predictors of student fear of school violence: A comparative study of eighth graders in 33 countries. *School Effectiveness and School Improvement, 19*(1), 51–72.

Akiba, M., LeTendre, G. K., & Scribner, J. P. (2007). Teacher quality, opportunity gap, and achievement gap in 47 countries. *Educational Researcher, 36*(7), 369–387.

American Federation of Teachers. (2002). *Transforming and modernizing family leave into leave with pay.* Retrieved June 15, 2008, from http://www.aft.org/about/resolutions/2002/family_leave.htm

American Federation of Teachers. (2007). *Survey and analysis of teacher salary trends 2005.* Washington, DC: Author.

Anderson-Levitt, K. (2003). *Local meanings, global schooling: Anthropology and world culture theory.* New York: Palgrave Macmillan.

Anderson-Levitt, K. (2005). The schoolyard gate: Schooling and childhood in global perspective. *Journal of Social History, 38*(4), 987–1006.

Arizona teacher working conditions survey. (n.d.). Retrieved August 12, 2008, from http://www.aztwc.org/

Ascher, C., & Fruchter, N. (2001). Teacher quality and student performance in New York City's low-performing schools. *Journal of Education for Students Placed at Risk, 6*(3), 199–214.

Australian Bureau of Statistics. (2006). *Schools Australia 2005* (Cat. No. 4221.0). Canberra, Australia: Author.

Australian Education Union. (2006). AEU national beginning teacher survey results 2006. Retrieved May 1, 2008, from http://www.aeufederal.org.au/Publications/Btsurvey06.html

Australian Government. (2008). *The Australian government quality teacher programme.* Retrieved May 1, 2008, from http://www.qualityteaching.dest.gov.au/about.htm

Baker, D., & LeTendre, G. (Eds.). (2005). *National differences, global similarities: World culture and the future of schooling.* Stanford, CA: Stanford University Press.

Benavot, A., & Braslavsky, C. (Eds.). (2006). *School knowledge in comparative and historical perspective: Changing curricula in primary and secondary education.* Hong Kong: Comparative Education Research Centre.

Benavot, A., Cha, Y., Kamens, D., Meyer, J., & Wong, S. (1991). Knowledge for the masses: World models and national curricula, 1920–1986. *American Sociological Review, 56*(1), 85–100.

Berliner, D., & Biddle, B. (1995). *The manufactured crisis.* New York: Addison-Wesley.

Birman, B. F., Le Floch, K. C., Klekotka, A., Ludwig, M., Taylor, J., Walters, K., et al. (2007). *State and local implementation of the No Child Left Behind Act: Vol. II. Teacher quality under NCLB: Interim report.* Washington, DC: U.S. Department of Education.

Blank, R. (2003). *Meeting NCLB goals for highly qualified teachers: Estimates by state from survey data.* Washington, DC: Council of Chief State School Officers.

Bonesronning, H., Falch, T., & Strom, B. (2005). Teacher sorting, teacher quality, and student composition. *European Economic Review, 49,* 457–483.

Borasi, R., & Fonzi, J. (2002). *Professional development that supports school mathematics reforms.* Arlington, VA: National Science Foundation.

Boyd, D., Grossman, P., Lankford, H., Loeb, S., & Wyckoff, J. (2006). How changes in entry requirements alter the teacher workforce and affect student achievement. *Education Finance and Policy, 1*(2), 176–215.

Breitsameter, F., Kissner, A., & Kordt, C. (2004). *PISA schnellkurs für erwachsene.* Munich, Germany: Compact.

Central Education Committee [Tyuo Kyoiku Shingikai]. (2007). *Kongono kyoin kyuyono arikatani tsuite* [Future plan for teacher salary]. Tokyo: Author.

Choy, S. P., Chen, X., & Bugarin, R. (2006). *Teacher professional development in 1999– 2000: What teachers, principals, and district staff report* (NCES 2006-305). Washington, DC: National Center for Education Statistics.

Clarke, D. (1994). Ten key principles from research on the professional development of mathematics teachers. In D. B. Aichele & A. F. Coxford (Eds.), *Professional development for teachers of mathematics* (pp. 37–48). Reston, VA: National Council of Teachers of Mathematics.

Clotfelter, C. T., Glennie, E., Ladd, H. F., & Vigdor, J. (2006). *Would higher salaries keep teachers in high-poverty schools? Evidence from a policy intervention in North Carolina* (NBER, Working Paper No. 12285). Cambridge, MA: National Bureau of Economic Research.

Coburn, C. (2006). Framing the problem of reading instruction: Using frame analysis to uncover the microprocesses of policy implementation. *American Educational Research Journal, 43,* 343–379.

Cohen, D. K., & Hill, H. C. (2000). Instructional policy and classroom performance: The mathematics reform in California. *Teachers College Record, 102*(2), 294–343.

Cohen, D. K., & Hill, H. C. (2001). *Learning policy: When state education reform works.* New Haven and London: Yale University Press.

Corcoran, T. B. (2007). The changing and chaotic world of teacher policy. In S. H. Fuhrman, D. K. Cohen & F. Mosher (Eds.), *The state of education policy research* (pp. 307–335). Mahwah, NJ: Erlbaum.

Darling-Hammond, L. (2004). Inequality and the right to learn: Access to qualified teachers in California's public schools. *Teachers College Record, 106*(10), 1936–1966.

Darling-Hammond, L. (2006). Securing the right to learn: Policy and practice for powerful teaching and learning. *Educational Researcher, 35*(7), 13–24.

Darling-Hammond, L. (2007). The flat earth and education: How America's commitment to equity will determine our future. *Educational Researcher, 36*(6), 318–334.

Darling-Hammond, L., & Sykes, G. (Eds.). (1999). *Teaching as the learning profession: Handbook of policy and practice.* San Francisco: Jossey-Bass.

Darling-Hammond, L., & Sykes, G. (2003). Wanted: A national teacher supply policy for education: The right way to meet the "highly qualified teacher" challenge. *Education Policy Analysis Archives, 11*(3). Retrieved May 15, 2008, from http://epaa.asu.edu/epaa/v11n33/

Darling-Hammond, L., & Sykes, G. (2004). A teacher supply policy for education: How to meet the "highly qualified teacher" challenge. In N. Epstein (Ed.), *Who's in charge here?* (pp. 164–227). Denver, CO: Education Commission of the States.

Darling-Hammond, L., & Youngs, P. (2002). Defining "highly qualified teachers": What does "scientifically-based research" actually tell us? *Educational Researcher, 31*(9), 13–25.

Department of Education, Employment and Workplace Relations, Commonwealth of Australia. (2008). *Teacher workforce data and planning processes in Australia.* Canberra, Australia: Authors.

Department of Education, Science and Training, Commonwealth of Australia. (2003). *Australia's teachers: Australia's future.* Canberra, Australia: Author.

Department of Education, Science and Training, Commonwealth of Australia. (2005). *An evaluation of the Australian government quality teacher programme 1999 to 2004.* Canberra, Australia: Author.

Department of Education, Science and Training, Commonwealth of Australia. (2007). *Annual report 2006–2007.* Canberra, Australia: Author.

Desimone, L. M., Porter, A. C., Garet, M. S., Yoon, K. S., & Birman, B. F. (2002). Effects of professional development on teachers' instruction: Results from a three-year longitudinal study. *Educational Evaluation and Policy Analysis, 24*(2), 81–112.

Dinham, S., Ingvarson, L., & Kleinhenz, E. (2008). *Investing in teacher quality: Doing what matters most.* Melbourne: Business Council of Australia.

Dougherty, K. (1996). Opportunity-to-learn standards: A sociological critique. *Sociology of Education, 69,* 40–65.

Dowling, A. (2007). *Australia's school funding system.* Camberwell, Australia: Australian Council for Educational Research.

Elmore, R. F. (2002). *Bridging the gap between standards and achievement: The imperative for professional development in education.* Washington, DC: Albert Shanker Institute.

Feiman-Nemser, S. (2001). From preparation to practice: Designing a continuum to strengthen and sustain teaching. *Teachers College Record, 103*(6), 1013–1055.

Fernandez, C., & Yoshida, M. (2004). *Lesson study: A Japanese approach to improving mathematics teaching and learning.* Mahwah, NJ: Erlbaum.

Fordham Foundation. (1999). *The teachers we need and how to get more of them.* Washington, DC: Author.

Fuhrman, S. H. (Ed.). (1993). *Designing coherent education policy: Improving the system.* San Francisco: Jossey-Bass.

Fuhrman, S. H., Goertz, M. E., & Weinbaum, E. H. (2007). Educational governance in the United States: Where are we? How did we get there? Why should we care? In S. H. Fuhrman, D. K. Cohen, & F. Mosher (Eds.), *The state of education policy research* (pp. 41–61). Mahwah, NJ: Erlbaum.

Fukuzawa, R., & LeTendre, G. (2001). *The intense years: How Japanese adolescents balance school, family, and friends.* New York: RoutledgeFalmer Press.

Garet, M. S., Porter, A. C., Desimone, L. M., Birman, B. F., & Yoon, K. S. (2001). What makes professional development effective? Results from a national sample of teachers. *American Educational Research Journal, 38*(4), 915–945.

Givvin, K., Hiebert, J., Jacobs, J., Hollingsworth, H., & Gallimore, R. (2005). Are there national patterns of teaching? Evidence from the TIMSS 1999 video study. *Comparative Education Review, 49*(3), 311–343.

Goddard, Y. L., Goddard, R. D., & Tschannen-Moran, M. (2007). A theoretical and empirical investigation of teacher collaboration for school improvement and student achievement in public elementary school. *Teachers College Record, 109*(4), 877–896.

Goldhaber, D. D., & Brewer, D. J. (1997). Why don't schools and teachers seem to matter? Assessing the impact of unobservables on educational productivity. *Journal of Human Resources, 32*(3), 505–523.

Goldhaber, D. D., & Brewer, D. J. (2000). Does teacher certification matter? High school teacher certification status and student achievement. *Educational Evaluation and Policy Analysis, 22*(2), 129–146.

Greenwald, R., Hedges, L. V., & Laine, R. D. (1996). The effect of school resources on student achievement. *Review of Educational Research, 66*(3), 361–396.

Grossman, P., & McDonald, M. (2008). Back to the future: Directions for research in teaching and teacher education. *American Educational Research Journal, 45*(1), 184–205.

Grossman, P., & Thompson, C. (2004). *Curriculum materials: Scaffolds for new teacher learning?* Seattle, WA: Center for the Study of Teaching and Policy.

Hampden-Thompson, G., Herring, W. L., & Kienzl, G. (2008). *Attrition of public school mathematics and science teachers.* Washington, DC: U.S. Department of Education.

Hanushek, E. A., Kain, J. F., & Rivkin, S. G. (2004). Why public schools lose teachers. *Journal of Human Resources, 39*(2), 326–354.

Hawley, W. D., & Valli, L. (1999). The essentials of effective professional development: A new consensus. In L. Darling-Hammond & G. Sykes (Eds.), *Teaching as the learning profession: Handbook of policy and practice* (pp. 127–150). San Francisco: Jossey-Bass.

Hiebert, J., Stigler, J. W., Jacobs, J. K., Givvin, K. B., Garnier, H., Smith, M. S., et al. (2005). Mathematics teaching in the United States today (and tomorrow): Results from the TIMSS 1999 video study. *Educational Evaluation and Policy Analysis, 27*(2), 111–132.

Hill, H. (2007). Mathematical knowledge of middle school teachers: Implications for the No Child Left Behind policy initiative. *Educational Evaluation and Policy Analysis, 29*(2), 95–114.

Hirsch, E. D. (1987). *Cultural literacy: What every American needs to know.* New York: Houghton Mifflin.

Howell, W. G., West, M. R., & Peterson, P. E. (2007). What Americans think about their schools? *Education Next, 7*(4), 12–26.

Humphrey, D., Wechsler, M., & Hough, H. (2008). Characteristics of effective alternative teacher certification programs. *Teachers College Record, 110*(1), 1–63.

Ibaraki Prefecture Teacher Union. (2007). *Tingin kenri tetyo* [Compensation and teacher rights handbook]. Ibaraki-ken, Japan: Author.

Ingersoll, R. M. (1996). *Out-of-field teaching and educational equality.* Washington, DC: National Center for Education Statistics.

Ingersoll, R. M. (1999). The problem of underqualified teachers in American secondary schools. *Educational Researcher, 28*(2), 26–37.

Ingersoll, R. M. (2001). Teacher turnover and teacher shortages. *American Educational Research Journal, 38*(3), 499–534.

Ingersoll, R. M. (2002). The teacher shortage: A case of wrong diagnosis and wrong prescription. *NASSP Bulletin, 86*(631), 16–31.

Ingersoll, R. M. (2003a). *Is there really a teacher shortage?* Seattle, WA: Center for the Study of Teaching and Policy.

Ingersoll, R. M. (2003b). *Who controls teachers' work?* Cambridge, MA: Harvard University Press.

Ingersoll, R. M. (2007). *A comparative study of teacher preparation and qualifications in six nations.* Philadelphia: Consortium for Policy Research in Education.

Ingvarson, L. (2002). *ACER policy briefs: Strengthening the profession? A comparison of recent reforms in the UK and the USA.* Camberwell, Australia: Australian Council for Educational Research.

Ingvarson, L., & Kleinhenz, E. (2003). *ACER policy briefs: A review of standards of practice for beginning teaching.* Camberwell, Australia: Australian Council for Educational Research.

Interstate New Teacher Assessment and Support Consortium. (1992). *Model standards for beginning teacher licensing, assessment and development: A resource for state dialogue.* Washington, DC: Author.

Jerald, C., & Ingersoll, R. M. (2002). *All talk, no action: Putting an end to out-of-field teaching.* Washington, DC: Education Trust. Retrieved November 15, 2006, from http://www.edtrust.org/main/documents/AllTalk.pdf

Johnson, S. M. (1990). *Teachers at work: Achieving success in our schools.* New York: Basic Books.

Johnson, S. M. (2006). *The workplace matters: Teacher quality, retention, and effectiveness.* Washington, DC: National Education Association.

Johnson, S. M., & The Project on the Next Generation of Teachers. (2004). *Finders and keepers: Helping new teachers survive and thrive in our schools.* San Francisco: Jossey-Bass.

Kansas teaching, learning and leadership survey. (n.d.). Retrieved August 12, 2008, from http://www.kantell.org/

Kardos, S. M. (2004). *Supporting and sustaining new teachers in schools: The importance of professional culture and mentoring.* Cambridge, MA: Harvard University Press.

Kauffman, D., Johnson, S. M., Kardos, S. M., Liu, E., & Peske, H. G. (2002). "Lost at sea": New teachers' experiences with curriculum and assessment. *Teachers College Record, 104*(2), 273–300.

Kozol, J. (1992). *Savage inequalities: Children in America's schools.* New York: Harper Perennial.

Kozol, J. (2005). *The shame of the nation: The restoration of apartheid schooling in America.* New York: Crown.

Kramer, R. (1991). *Ed school follies: The miseducation of America's teachers.* New York: Free Press.

Kushman, J. W. (1992). The organizational dynamics of teacher workplace commitment: A study of urban elementary and middle schools. *Educational Administration Quarterly, 28*(1), 5–42.

Labaree, D. (2004). *The trouble with ed schools.* New Haven, CT: Yale University Press.

Ladson-Billings, G. (2006). From the achievement gap to the education debt: Understanding achievement in U.S. schools. *Educational Researcher, 35*(10), 3–12.

Lauder, H., Brown, P., Dillabough, J., & Halsey, A. H. (2006). *Education, globalization and social change.* London: Oxford University Press.

Lee, S., & Zusho, A. (2002). Comparing Japanese and U.S. teachers' manuals: Implications for mathematics teaching and learning. In G. DeCoker (Ed.), *National standards and school reform in Japan and the United States* (pp. 67–91). New York: Teachers College Press.

LeTendre, G. (1994). Guiding them on: Teaching, hierarchy, and social organization in Japanese middle schools. *Journal of Japanese Studies, 20*(1), 37–59.

LeTendre, G. (1995). Disruption and reconnection: Counseling young adolescents in Japanese schools. *Educational Policy, 9*(2), 169–184.

LeTendre, G. (Ed.). (1999). *Competitor or ally: Japan's role in American educational debates.* New York: Falmer Press.

LeTendre, G. (2000). *Learning to be adolescent: Growing up in U.S. and Japanese middle schools.* New Haven, CT: Yale University Press.

LeTendre, G., & Akiba, M. (2001). Teacher beliefs about adolescent development: Cultural and organizational impacts on Japanese and U.S. middle school teachers' beliefs. *Compare, 31*(2), 187–203.

LeTendre, G., & Akiba, M. (2005). Schoolwork at home? Low-quality schooling and homework. In D. Baker & G. LeTendre (Eds.), *National differences, global similarities: World culture and the future of schooling* (pp. 117–133). Stanford, CA: Stanford University Press.

LeTendre, G., Baker, D., Akiba, M., Goesling, B., & Wiseman, A. (2001a). Teachers' work: Institutional isomorphism and cultural variation in the U.S., Germany and Japan. *Educational Researcher, 30*(6), 3–15.

LeTendre, G., Baker, D., Akiba, M., & Wiseman, A. (2001b). The policy trap: National educational policy and the Third International Math and Science Study. *International Journal of Educational Policy Research and Practice, 2*(1), 45–64.

Levin, J., & Quinn, M. (2003). *Missed opportunities: How we keep high-quality teachers out of urban classrooms.* New York: The New Teacher Project.

Lewis, C. (1995). *Educating hearts and mind: Reflections on Japanese preschool and elementary education.* Cambridge: Cambridge University Press.

Lewis, C. (2002a). Does lesson study have a future in the United States? *Nagoya Journal of Education and Human Development, 1,* 1–23.

Lewis, C. (2002b). *Lesson study: A handbook for teacher-led instructional change.* Philadelphia: Research for Better Schools.

Lewis, C., Perry, R., & Hurd, J. (2004). A deeper look at lesson study. *Educational Leadership, 61*(5), 18–22.

Lewis, C., Perry, R., Hurd, J., & O'Connell, M. P. (2006). Lesson study comes of age in North America. *Phi Delta Kappan, 88(4),* 273–281.

Lewis, C., & Tsuchida, I. (1997). Planned educational change in Japan: The shift to student-centered elementary science. *Journal of Education Policy, 12*(5), 313–331.

Lewis, C., & Tsuchida, I. (1998). A lesson is like a swiftly flowing river: Research lessons and the improvement of Japanese education. *American Educator, 22*(4), 14–17, 50–52.

Lewis, C., Tsuchida, I., & Coleman, S. (2002). The creation of Japanese and U.S. elementary science textbooks: Different processes, different outcomes. In G. DeCoker (Ed.), *National standards and school reform in Japan and the United States* (pp. 35–45). New York: Teachers College Press.

Ling, L. M., Chik, P., & Pang, M. F. (2006). Patterns of variation in teaching the colour of light to primary 3 students. *Instructional Science: An International Journal of Learning and Cognition, 34*(1), 1–19.

Linn, M. C., Lewis, C., Tsuchida, I., & Songer, N. B. (2000). Beyond fourth-grade science: Why do U.S. and Japanese students diverge? *Educational Researcher, 29*(3), 4–14.

Little, J. W. (1999). Organizing schools for teacher learning. In L. Darling-Hammond & G. Sykes (Eds.), *Teaching as the learning profession: Handbook of policy and practice* (pp. 233–262). San Francisco: Jossey-Bass.

Liu, E., & Johnson, S. M. (2006). New teachers' experiences of hiring: Late, rushed, and information-poor. *Educational Administration Quarterly, 42*(3), 324–360.

Loucks-Horsley, S., Hewson, P. W., Love, N., & Stiles, K. E. (1998). *Designing professional development for teachers of science and mathematics.* Thousand Oaks, CA: Corwin Press.

Manuel, J. (2003). "Such are the ambitions of youth": Exploring issues of retention and attrition of early career teachers in New South Wales. *Asia-Pacific Journal of Teacher Education, 31*(2), 140–151.

Marvel, J., Lyter, D. M., Peltola, P., Strizek, G. A., & Morton, B. A. (2006*). Teacher attrition and mobility: Results from the 2004–2005 teacher follow-up survey* (NCES 2007-307). Washington, DC: National Center for Education Statistics.

McCormack, A., Gore, J., & Thomas, K. (2006). Early career teacher professional learning. *Asia-Pacific Journal of Teacher Education, 34*(1), 95–113.

McCormack, A., & Thomas, K. (2003). Is survival enough? Induction experiences of beginning teachers within a New South Wales context. *Asia-Pacific Journal of Teacher Education, 31*(2), 125–138.

McKenzie, P., Kos, J., Walker, M., & Hong, J. (2008). *Staff in Australia's schools 2007.* Canberra, Australia: Commonwealth of Australia.

McKinsey & Company. (2007). *How the world's best-performing school systems come out on top.* New York: Author.

McLaughlin, M. W., & Talbert, J. E. (2006). *Building school-based teacher learning communities: Professional strategies to improve student achievement.* New York and London: Teachers College Press.

Meyer, J., Ramirez, F., & Soysal, Y. N. (1992). World expansion of mass education, 1870–1980. *Sociology of Education, 65*(2), 128–149.

Ministerial Council on Education, Employment, Training and Youth Affairs. (1999). *Adelaide declaration on national goals for schooling in the 21st century.* Retrieved March 1, 2008, from http://www.mceetya.edu.au/mceetya/nationalgoals/index.htm

Ministerial Council on Education, Employment, Training and Youth Affairs. (2003). *A national framework for professional standards for teaching.* Carlton South Victoria, Australia: Author.

Ministerial Council on Education, Employment, Training and Youth Affairs. (2005). *Demand and supply of primary and secondary teachers in Australia.* Melbourne: Author.

Ministerial Council on Education, Employment, Training and Youth Affairs. (2006). *National report on schooling in Australia: Preliminary paper.* Carlton South Victoria, Australia: Author.

Ministerial Council on Education, Employment, Training and Youth Affairs. (2008). *Statements of learning.* Retrieved March 1, 2008, from http://www.mceetya.edu.au/mceetya/statements_of_learning,22835.html

Ministry of Education, Culture, Sports, Science and Technology (MEXT). (1999). *Kyouin no kaku raifu sute-ji ni oujite motomerareru shishitu nouryoku* [Teacher quality and competence required for each professional life stage]. Tokyo: Author.

Ministry of Education, Culture, Sports, Science and Technology. (2006). *Kyouin hogosya ishiki tyousa* [Teacher and family opinion survey]. Tokyo: Author.

Ministry of Education, Culture, Sports, Science and Technology. (2007a). *Gakko kihon tyosa 2005* [School basic statistics 2005]. Tokyo: Author.

Ministry of Education, Culture, Sports, Science and Technology. (2007b). *Juunen keikeinsya kenshu jisshi joukyou tyousa kekka* [Tenth-year teacher professional development survey results]. Tokyo: Author.

Ministry of Education, Culture, Sports, Science and Technology. (2007c). *Kyoin kinmu jittai tyousak zantei shukei* [Teacher working conditions survey results]. Tokyo: Author.

Ministry of Education, Culture, Sports, Science and Technology. (2007d). *Shoninsya kenshu jisshi joukyou tyousa kekka* [First-year teacher induction program implementation survey results]. Tokyo: Author.

Ministry of Education, Culture, Sports, Science and Technology. (2007e). *Zenkokugakuryoku gakushu joukyo tyousa* [National achievement and learning assessment]. Tokyo: Author.

Ministry of Education, Culture, Sports, Science and Technology. (2008a). *Gakko tyosa ni tsuite* [School evaluation system]. Retrieved May 1, 2008, from http://www.mext.go.jp/a_menu/shotou/gakko-hyoka/index.htm

Ministry of Education, Culture, Sports, Science and Technology. (2008b). *Miryokuaru kyoinwo motomete* [Seeking attractive teachers]. Tokyo: Author.

Monk, D. (2008). Reflections and commentary from the field: Connecting the reform of administrator preparation to the reform of teacher preparation. *Educational Administration Quarterly, 44*(2), 282–295.

Moon, B. (2007). *Research analysis: Attracting, developing and retaining effective teachers: A global overview of current policies and practices.* Paris: UNESCO.

Nakamoto, T. (2008). Konna sensei motomemasu. Zen 64 todohuken seireitoshino kyoikutyo karano messegi [We are looking for a teacher who is . . . : Messages from the 64 chairs of prefecture boards of education]. *Teaching Profession Course, 34*(10), 41–65.

National Academies. (2007). *Study of teacher preparation programs in the United States.* Retrieved December 1, 2006, from http://www7.nationalacademies.org/teacherprep/

National Board for Professional Teaching Standards. (1994). *What teachers should know and be able to do.* Retrieved January 15, 2009, from www.nbpts.org/UserFiles/File/what_teachers.pdf

National Board for Professional Teaching Standards. (n.d.). Raising the standards. Retrieved July 3, 2008, from http://www.nbpts.org/about_us/mission_and_history/milestones

National Center for Education Statistics. (2007). *Digest of Education Statistics: 2007.* Washington, DC: Author.

National Center for Education Statistics. (2008a). *Highlights from PISA 2006.* Washington, DC: Author.

National Center for Education Statistics. (2008b). *SASS 2003–04 public school teacher file.* Retrieved July 3, 2008, from http://www.nces.ed.gov/dasolv2/index.asp

National Commission on Excellence in Education. (1983). *A Nation at Risk: The Imperative for Educational Reform.* Washington, DC: Author.

National Commission on Teaching and America's Future. (1996). *What matters most: Teaching for America's future.* New York: Author.

National Commission on Teaching and America's Future. (2003). *No dream denied: A pledge to America's children.* New York: Author.

National Council on Teacher Quality. (2006). *Benefits.* Retrieved June 3, 2008, from http://www.nctq.org/tr3/issues/index.jsp?sectionId=3

National Institute of Education, Singapore. (2007). Research areas. Retrieved June 11, 2008, from http://www.nie.edu.sg/nieweb/dept/loading.do?id=Academic &cid=22052866&ppid=23199750

Neild, R. C., Useem, E., Travers, E. F., & Lesnick, J. (2003). *Once and for all: Placing a high quality teacher in every Philadelphia classroom.* Philadelphia: Research for Action.

New South Wales Department of Education and Training. (2003). *Leave provisions.* Sydney: Author.

New South Wales Department of Education and Training. (2008). *Employment with us.* Retrieved May 1, 2008, from https://www.det.nsw.edu.au/employment/teachnsw/index.htm

New South Wales Institute of Teachers. (2006). *Information for new scheme teachers.* Sydney: Author.

New South Wales Institute of Teachers. (n.d.a). *Professional teaching standards.* Sydney: Author.

New South Wales Institute of Teachers. (n.d.b). *Your continuing professional development: Supporting you to maintain your accreditation at the level of professional competence.* Sydney: Author.

North Carolina teacher working conditions survey. (n.d.). Retrieved August 12, 2008, from http://www.ncptsc.org:80/index.htm

Northern Territory Government. (2008). *Work conditions and benefits.* Retrieved June 11, 2008, from http://www.teaching.nt.gov.au/index.cfm?attributes.fuseaction=workAndLive#work

Olmsted, P., & Weikert, D. (Eds.). (1989). *How nations serve young children: Profiles of child care and education in 14 countries.* Ypsilanti, MI: High/Scope Press.

Organisation for Economic Co-operation and Development. (2004). *The quality of the teaching workforce.* Paris: Author.

Organisation for Economic Co-operation and Development. (2005). *Teachers matter: Attracting, developing and retaining effective teachers.* Paris: Author.

Organisation for Economic Co-operation and Development. (2007). *Education at a glance 2007.* Paris: Author.

Osborn, M., Broadfoot, P., McNess, E., Planel, C., Ravn, B., & Triggs, P. (2003). *A world of difference? Comparing learners across Europe.* Maidenhead, UK: Open University Press.

Ota, N. (2000). Teacher education and its reform in contemporary Japan. *International Studies in Sociology of Education, 10*(1), 43–59.

Peckham, S. (2007). Association of teacher educators supports lawsuit on teacher quality. *The Education Digest, 73*(4), 74–76.

Peske, H. G., & Haycock, K. (2006). *Teaching inequality: How poor and minority students are shortchanged on teacher quality.* Washington, DC: Education Trust.

Prenzel, M., Baumert, J., & Blum, W. (2005). *PISA 2003 Der zweite vergleich der länder in Deutschland—Was wissen und können Jugendliche?* Berlin: Waxmann.

Provasnik, S., & Dorfman, S. (2005). *Mobility in the teaching workforce* (NCES 2005-114). Washington, DC: National Center for Education Statistics.

Quality counts 2008: The teaching profession. (2008). Education Week. Retrieved June 11, 2008, from http://www.edweek.org/media/ew/qc/2008/18sos.h27.teaching.pdf

Queensland Department of Education, Training and the Arts. (2008). *Guide for teacher applicants*. Retrieved May 15, 2008, from http://education.qld.gov.au/hr/recruitment/apply/pdfs/guide-to-teacher-employment-08.pdf

Ramirez, F. O., & Boli, J. (1987). The political construction of mass schooling: European origin and worldwide institutionalization. *Sociology of Education, 60*(1), 2–17.

Rice, J. K. (2003). *Teacher quality: Understanding the effectiveness of teacher attributes.* Washington, DC: Economic Policy Institute.

Rivkin, S., Hanushek, E., & Kain, J. (2005). Teachers, schools and academic achievement. *Econometrica, 73*(2), 417–458.

Rotherham, A., & Mead, S. (2004). Back to the future: The history and politics of state teacher licensure and certification. In F. Hess, A. Rotherham, & K. Walsh (Eds.), *A qualified teacher in every classroom?* (pp. 41–61). Cambridge, MA: Harvard Education Press.

Rowan, B., Chiang, F., & Miller, R. J. (1997). Using research on employees' performance to study the effects of teachers on students' achievement. *Sociology of Education, 70*(4), 256–284.

Sable, J., & Hill, J. (2006). *Overview of public elementary and secondary students, staff, schools, school districts, revenues, and expenditures: School year 2004–05 and fiscal year 2004* (NCES 2007-309). Washington, DC: National Center for Education Statistics.

Schmidt, W., Houang, R. T., & Cogan, L. (2002, Summer). A coherent curriculum. *American Educator, 26*, 1–17.

Schmidt, W. H., McKnight, C. C., Houang, R. T., Wang, H., Wiley, D. E., Cogan, L. S., et al. (2001). *Why schools matter: A cross-national comparison of curriculum and learning.* San Francisco: Jossey-Bass.

Schmidt, W. H., Tatto, M. T., Bankov, K., Blomeke, S., Cedillo, T., Cogan, L., et al. (2007). *The preparation gap: Teacher education for middle school mathematics in six countries.* East Lansing: MI: Center for Research in Mathematics and Science Education.

Shen, J., Mansberger, N. B., & Yang, H. (2004). Teacher quality and students placed at risk: Results from the Baccalaureate and Beyond Longitudinal Study, 1993–97. *Educational Horizons, 82*(3), 226–235.

Shimahara, N. K. (2002). Teacher professional development in Japan. In G. DeCoker (Ed.), *National standards and school reform in Japan and the United States* (pp. 107–120). New York: Teachers College Press.

Shimahara, N. K., & Sakai, A. (1995). *Learning to teach in two cultures: Japan and United States.* New York and London: Garland.

Shimizu, K., Akao, K., Atai, A., Ito, T., & Sato, H., et al. (2006). *Saishin kyouiku detabukku* [Databook of educational statistics]. Tokyo: Jijitsushinsya.

Sipple, J., Killeen, K., & Monk, D. (2004). Adoption and adaptation: School district responses to state imposed learning and graduation requirements. *Educational Evaluation and Policy Analysis, 26*(2), 143–168.

Skilbeck, M., & Connell, H. (2004). *Teachers for the future: The changing nature of society and related issues for the teaching workforce.* Carlton South Victoria, Australia: Ministerial Council for Education, Employment, Training and Youth Affairs.

Smith, T. M. (2007). How do state-level induction and standards-based reform policies affect induction experiences and turnover among new teachers? *American Journal of Education, 113*, 273–309.

Smith, T. M., Desimone, L. M., & Ueno, K. (2005). "Highly qualified" to do what? The relationship between NCLB teacher quality mandates and the use of reform-oriented instruction in middle school mathematics. *Educational Evaluation and Policy Analysis, 27*(1), 75–109.

Smith, T. M., & Ingersoll, R. M. (2004). What are the effects of induction and mentoring on beginning teacher turnover? *American Educational Research Journal, 41*, 681–714.

Smith, M. S., & O'Day, J. (1991). Systemic school reform. In S. H. Fuhrman & B. Malen (Eds.), *The politics of curriculum and testing* (pp. 233–267). New York: Falmer Press.

Smylie, M. A., & Miretzky, D. (Eds.). (2004). *Developing the teacher workforce.* Chicago: University of Chicago Press.

Spillane, J. P. (2004). *Standards deviation: How schools misunderstand education policy.* Cambridge, MA: Harvard University Press.

Stein, S. (2004). *The culture of educational policy.* New York: Teachers College Press.

Steiner-Khamsi, G. (1999). Teacher education reform. *Comparative Education Review, 43*(3), 353–361.

Steiner-Khamsi, G. (2004). *The global politics of educational borrowing and lending.* New York and London: Teachers College Press.

Stigler, J. W., & Hiebert, J. (1999). *The teaching gap: Best ideas from the world's teachers for improving education in the classroom.* New York: Free Press.

Strizek, G. A., Pittsonberger, J. L., Riordan, K. E., Lyter, D. M., & Orlofsky, G. F. (2006). *Characteristics of schools, districts, teachers, principals, and school libraries in the United States: 2003–04 Schools and Staffing Survey* (NCES 2006–313 Rev.). Washington, DC: National Center for Education Statistics.

Struck, P. (2008). *Die 15 gebote des lernens. Schule nach PISA.* Darmstadt, Germany: Primus Verlag.

Suarez-Orozco, M., & Qin-Hilliard, D. B. (2004). *Globalization: Culture and education in the new millennium.* Berkeley: University of California Press.

Tasmania Department of Education. (2007). *Beginning teacher time release program (BeTTR).* Retrieved June 11, 2008, from http://www.education.tas.gov.au/dept/employment/teachers/tasmania/bettr

Tasmania Department of Education. (2008a). *Graduate recruitment program.* Retrieved May 1, 2008, from http://www.education.tas.gov.au/dept/employment/teachers/gradrecruitment

Tasmania Department of Education. (2008b). *Professional experience in isolated and rural schools (PEIRS).* Retrieved May 1, 2008, from http://www.education.tas.gov.au/dept/employment/teachers/peirs

Tatto, M. (2007). International comparisons and the global reform of teaching. In M. T. Tatto (Ed.), *Reforming Teaching Globally* (pp. 7–18). Oxford, England: Symposium Books.

Teaching Australia. (2007). *A proposal for a national system for the accreditation of preservice teacher education.* Acton ACT, Australia: Author.

Teaching Australia. (2008). *National professional standards for advanced teaching and for principals: Second consultation paper.* Acton ACT, Australia: Author.

Teaching Commission. (2004). *Teaching at risk: A call to action.* New York: Author.

Teaching Commission. (2006). *Teaching at risk: Progress and potholes.* New York: Author.

TIMSS & PIRLS International Study Center. (2006). *TIMSS 2003 highlights.* Chestnut Hill, MA: Boston College.

Tobin, J. J., Wu, D. Y., & Davidson, D. H. (1989). *Preschool in three cultures: Japan, China, and the United States.* New Haven and London: Yale University Press.

Tsuneyoshi, R. (2004). The new Japanese educational reforms and the achievement "crisis" debate. *Educational Policy, 18,* 364–394.

UNESCO Institute for Statistics. (2006). *Teachers and educational quality: Monitoring global needs for 2015.* Montreal, Canada: Author.

UNESCO Institute for Statistics. (2008). *UIS statistics in brief.* Montreal, Canada: Author.

U.S. Department of Education. (2006). *The secretary's fifth annual report on teacher quality: A highly qualified teacher in every classroom.* Washington, DC: Author.

U.S. Department of Education. (2008a). *Improving teacher quality state grants.* Retrieved May 8, 2008, from http://www.ed.gov/programs/teacherqual/index.html

U.S. Department of Education. (2008b). Key policy letters signed by the education secretary or deputy secretary. Retrieved August 12, 2008, from http://www.ed.gov/policy/elsec/guid/secletter/080403.html

Victoria Department of Education and Training. (2008a). *Allowances.* Retrieved June 8, 2008, from http://www.education.vic.gov.au/hrweb/employcond/allow/Default.htm

Victoria Department of Education and Training. (2008b). *Career change program.* Retrieved May 10, 2008, from http://www.teaching.vic.gov.au/news/careerchg/default.htm

Victoria Department of Education and Training. (2008c). *Leave.* Retrieved June 8, 2008, from http://www.education.vic.gov.au/hrweb/employcond/leave/default.htm

Victoria Department of Education and Training. (2008d). *Teaching scholarships.* Retrieved May 10, 2008, from http://www.teaching.vic.gov.au/news/scholarship/default.htm

Victorian Institute of Teaching. (2008). *Mentoring keeps regional teachers at top of the class.* Retrieved June 11, 2008, from http://www.vit.vic.edu.au/files/documents/1456_VIT-MENTORING-REGIONAL-RURAL.pdf

Victorian Institute of Teaching. (n.d.). *Professional learning.* Retrieved July 15, 2008, from http://www.vit.vic.edu.au/content.asp?Document_ID=871

Walberg, H. (1998). *Spending more while learning less.* Washington, DC: Fordham Foundation.

Wang, A. H., Coleman, A. B., Coley, R. J., & Phelps, R. P. (2003). *Preparing teachers around the world.* Princeton, NJ: Educational Testing Service.

Wang, J. (1998). Opportunity to learn: The impacts and policy implications. *Educational Evaluation and Policy Analysis, 20*(3), 137–156.

Wayne, A. J., & Youngs, P. (2003). Teacher characteristics and student achievement gains: A review. *Review of Educational Research, 73*(1), 89–122.

Welmond, M. (2002). Globalization viewed from the periphery: The dynamics of teacher identity in the Republic of Benin. *Comparative Education Review, 46*(1), 37–65.

Western Australia Department of Education and Training. (2008a). *Holidays and leave entitlements.* Retrieved June 8, 2008, from http://www.det.wa.edu.au/teachingwa/detcms/navigation/student-teachers/the-teaching-profession/holidays-and-leave-entitlements/

Western Australia Department of Education and Training. (2008b). *Rural teaching program.* Retrieved May 10, 2008, from http://www.det.wa.edu.au/teachingwa/detcms/navigation/student-teachers/rural-teaching-program/

Wilson, S. M., & Berne, J. (1999). Teacher learning and the acquisition of professional knowledge: An examination of research on contemporary professional development. *Review of Research in Education, 24,* 173–209.

Wilson, S. M., Darling-Hammond, L., & Berry, B. (2001). *A case of successful teaching policy: Connecticut's long-term efforts to improve teaching and learning.* Seattle, WA: Center for the Study of Teaching and Policy.

Wilson, S. M., Floden, R. E., & Ferrini-Mundy, J. (2001). *Teacher preparation research: Current knowledge, gaps, and recommendations.* Seattle, WA: Center for the Study of Teaching and Policy.

Wilson, S. M., Floden, R. E., & Ferrini-Mundy, J. (2002). Teacher preparation research: An insider's view from the outside. *Journal of Teacher Education, 53*(3), 190–204.

Zeng, K. (1999). *Dragon gate: Competitive examinations and their consequences.* New York: Continuum International.

About the Authors

Motoko Akiba is an assistant professor in the Department of Educational Leadership and Policy Analysis at the University of Missouri–Columbia. She received a BA in education from the University of Tsukuba, Japan, a Ph.D. in educational theory and policy, and a dual-title Ph.D. in comparative and international education from Pennsylvania State University–University Park. Before joining MU, she was a senior researcher at Mid-continent Research for Education and Learning (McREL). She conducts policy research on teacher quality and learning, multicultural teacher education, and school safety using both U.S. and international data. Specifically, she takes a comparative and international approach to examining teacher policy issues that influence student learning and behavior. She received the Isabelle Lyda Professorship for outstanding research accomplishment in 2005, Outstanding Reviewer Award from the *American Educational Research Journal* in 2007, and the National Science Foundation CAREER award in 2008. She currently serves on the editorial boards of the *American Educational Research Journal* (*Social and Institutional Analysis*) and the *American Journal of Education*. With the NSF CAREER award grant, she is leading a 5-year project that examines teachers' work contexts and learning opportunities using longitudinal survey and case study methods.

Gerald K. LeTendre, Professor of Education and International Affairs, is chair of the Educational Policy Studies Department at Pennsylvania State University. He currently is editor of the *American Journal of Education* and serves on the editorial board of the *Comparative Education Review*. He received his BA (magna cum laude) in sociology from Harvard University and was awarded a Rockefeller Fellowship to do fieldwork among Tibetan refugees. He completed his graduate work at Stanford University where he received an MA in sociology and a Ph.D. in education. He has been the recipient of a Japan Foundation Fellowship, a Johann Jacobs Young Scholar Award, and a Spencer Post-doctoral Fellowship, and was a Fulbright Senior Scholar at the University of Bremen in Germany (2003–04). He has published on a broad range of topics in comparative and international education, including the articles "What Is Tracking? Cultural Expectations in the U.S., Germany and Japan" (*American Educational Research Journal*) and "The Policy Trap: National Educational Policy and the Third International Math and Science Study" (*International Journal of Educational Policy Research and Practice*). His most recent books include *National Differences, Global Similarities: World Culture and the Future of Schooling* (with David Baker), *Learning to Be Adolescent: Growing up in U.S. and Japanese Middle Schools*, and *Intense Years: How Japanese Adolescents Balance School, Family and Friends* (with Becky Fukuzawa). His current research interests include changing work roles for teachers cross-nationally and the diffusion of prevention programs in schools worldwide.

Index